BLOOD BARRIOS

Dispatches from the World's Deadliest Streets

ALBERTO ARCE

**TRANSLATED BY JOHN WASHINGTON
AND DANIELA UGAZ**

Illustrated by Germán Andino

ENGLISH PEN

ARTS COUNCIL
ENGLAND

Supported using public funding by
ARTS COUNCIL
ENGLAND

ZED

This edition of *Blood Barrios: Dispatches from the World's Deadliest Streets*
was published in 2018 by Zed Books Ltd,
The Foundry, 17 Oval Way, London SE11 5RR, UK.

www.zedbooks.net

English language translation © Daniela Ugaz and John Washington, 2017.

Copyright for the text © Alberto Arce, 2015.
Copyright for the illustrations © Germán Andino, 2015.

Originally published in Spanish by Libros del KO in 2015.

This translation is published by arrangement with Oh! Books Agencia Literaria.

*This book has been selected to receive financial assistance from English PEN's
"PEN Translates" programme, supported by Arts Council England. English PEN
exists to promote literature and our understanding of it, to uphold writers' freedoms
around the world, to campaign against the persecution and imprisonment of writers
for stating their views, and to promote the friendly co-operation of writers
and the free exchange of ideas. www.englishpen.org*

The rights of Alberto Arce to be identified as the author of this work have been
asserted by him in accordance with the Copyright, Designs and Patents Act, 1988.

Typeset in Haarlemmer by seagulls.net
Cover design by David A. Gee

A catalogue record for this book is available from the British Library

ISBN 978-1-78699-049-5 pb
ISBN 978-1-78699-051-8 pdf
ISBN 978-1-78699-052-5 epub
ISBN 978-1-78699-053-2 mobi

MIX
Paper from
responsible sources
FSC
www.fsc.org   FSC® C020471

CONTENTS

Part IV: The Police

Part V: Storytellers

ACKNOWLEDGMENTS

What helped me endure so long in Honduras was my constant desire to return home to see Sarah and Selma.

I want to thank the three editors of Associated Press, Marjorie Miller, Trish Wilson, and Katherine Corcoran, who gave me the opportunity, the means, the time, and the resources to cover for almost three years the events of a country that, in theory, matters to no one.

"So, when we all, all of us, have killed one another, and between Guatemala and Nicaragua nothing is left but one hideous and solitary puddle of blood, these texts may help the countries of the future not turn out like us..."

(Juan Martínez)

In the last fifty years, Central Americans have survived twelve coups d'état, one successful revolution and two failed revolutions, four declared wars, one genocide, one American invasion, eighteen hurricanes, and eight earthquakes. To the 320,000 dead from the wars of the 1980s we add 180,000 homicides. Most of these occurred in Honduras, where more than 55,000 people have been murdered in the last decade.

Routes of cocaine and violence in Honduras

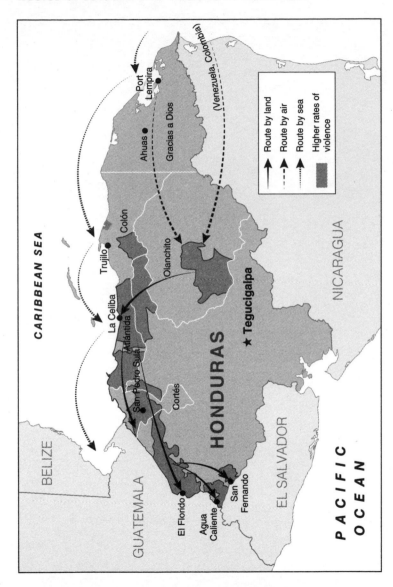

PART I

RED JOURNALISM

1

INSIDE THE VOLCANO

You'll notice the delicate pink flowers of the bougainvillea crawling over the cobblestoned street corners, the dusty mudbrick of the adobe, and the red tiles of the colorful houses, but only if you can get your head out of the volcano.

Living in Teguz is like drowning inside a volcano. In Tegucicrater—as some of us call it when there are no Hondurans around to hear us—you leave your house at six in the evening, you have your daughter's tricycle wedged under your arm, and, on the street corner in Parque de la Leona, you approach the small group of people gathered around a dead body. You smell the blood; you coolly look at the bullet hole stamped into the head—you've learned to contain your nausea—and you begin, without your notebook, to ask questions, just out of curiosity, just as a citizen. No one can live in a place for two years without feeling a part of it.

To get your head out of the volcano you have to pierce through the hills of trash and the dogs that live in them, the invasive labyrinth of electrical cables and bootlegged wiring, the car exhaust, the pervasive sound of the cityscape, and the night that falls like a blanket over streets without lampposts or traffic lights. As you lift your head you'll start to notice changes in the weather, the rain. By this point you've learned to hurry to beat the mudslide that will soon flood the neighborhood, to stick a hand out of the window to wave on the taxi behind you, and to drive on through the night with the anxiety of a junkie in search of one of the few gasoline stations that sell Marlboro Reds.

To exist here you have to learn to live with fear, rage, boredom, impotence, and frustration. The boredom of interviewing politicians and bureaucrats, the frustration that in a country where a woman is murdered every twenty hours, the half-dozen protesters gathered at a feminist rally can't agree on what their banner should read. The anger of seeing a boy drop out of school to push a squeaking ice cream cart eight hours a day. The impotence of thinking about that girl who was shot in the leg by her dad, but who doesn't want to go to the hospital because they might report the accident— the accident that happened when he, a police officer, was cleaning his gun while waiting for dinner to be ready after a 72-hour shift.

To survive the volcano, I've learned to protect myself against the ugly. I don't need Google glasses; I only need my time machine. In the dead hours of a traffic jam, I've learned to imagine the city in black and white. Dozens of times,

I've dreamed of the Teguz of the 1940s, 1950s, and 1960s, with its colonial houses, its gossiping crowds huddled at a church entrance, its billiards, its political hangouts, like the barbershop where Kapuscinski would get a straight shave before waiting in line to send a telegram, and where old men still sit to while away the hours, the type of men who touch the brims of their sombreros to greet passersby.

Most foreign journalists don't pass the first cut, not even with the generous hazard-tax they can charge; they throw in the towel, leaving behind a defeated city where even party streamers are made of rusty barbed wire. Nicaragua, just a few hours away by car, is too close to Honduras to seem a legitimate place of refuge, and correspondents (myself included) lack the intimacy—the political or religious will—to live in Honduras without being Honduran. But those of us who make the cut—those of us who think we've made the cut—we fight it out together in our Central American Melrose Place. In the *Giraldilla*, protected and surrounded by eucalyptus and guava trees, by squirrels, and by the aloe vera that covers the wall separating us from the streets, and protected by Lucas, a father of eleven children who doesn't know how to read or write, but who, with a machete in hand, guards over us night after night.

Lucas heats up a can of beans and a tortilla over burning embers in the yard; he makes less in a month than we spend on a Saturday night out on the town—we who party and love to talk about social justice, and yet refuse to open our door on a cold night lest Lucas come by to ask us for a little extra money for medication, or because his wallet's been stolen. Nor do we open the door to the million people living just outside, a stone's throw from the few houses remaining in the upper district. Many, in any given moment of bad luck, would kill us for what we have in our pockets. They don't do it, though, because we don't expose ourselves. Because we don't step onto their streets or into their markets, and we think that, in this way, they'll never reach us. The night I write this, however, the dead man, Don Esteban, a taxi driver with Parkinson's, was left slumped with a bullet hole between his eyes on the same street corner I stand on every day while waiting for my driver.

For a reporter who likes both the mud and the lava, this place is basically a rave. Ecstasy comes by way of a hunk of flesh and a spurt of blood. Like the modern mother who swallows pills made out of her own placenta, we reporters seek out the dead bodies to harden ourselves. My neighbor, Germán (the illustrator of this book) dropped his notebook as he was sketching a crime scene, staining it in blood. The blood soaked into the paper, staining it, just like the spurts of machine gun fire soiled our Sunday evening cocktail party a few days before. Yesterday, when Don Esteban, shot dead, slumped over the steering wheel of his taxi, we could only think of one thing: "There's nothing more to tell here."

Tegucigalpa is a city where you don't complain about somebody cutting you off in the street. Especially if that person is driving a double-cab pickup without plates. It's a city where you don't go looking for what you don't want to find. Where you buy beer at the corner market and can feel the fear emanating from Gladys, the cashier who, despite having known you for a year, now only talks to you from behind metal bars, speedily snatching your two dollars before handing you your groceries. Where, when you turn around, beers in hand, you see a fifty-year-old man in rags sitting on a stack of Coca-Cola bottles in the back of a delivery truck, wearing a cheap bulletproof vest and holding a loaded shotgun at the ready. Where the same scene repeats itself on an egg delivery truck. Where they kill these guards to rob them of their shotguns, which cost less than a day's wages. Where the businessmen making money from these robberies are also army colonels or chiefs of police. Where my daughter, just a year and a half old, sees a dead body for the first time and knows that something's different, that I'm trying to hide something from her, that the body we walk by is a dead body, and not a man taking a nap.

This is a country where the president goes on national TV, interrupting regular programming on every channel, to denounce the high-profile businessmen who import, tax-free, French mineral water they claim is necessary for their health. He doesn't name the businessmen, or file any charges, and certainly he doesn't change the laws that he himself approved, which allow the tax-free imports in the first place. The announcement is just his way of extorting the businessmen so they'll help fund his next campaign.

Honduras is a country where nobody has ever seen a mailman or a place to buy stamps, and yet UNICEF released a series of stamps to promote children's rights, and, one Thursday afternoon, you receive an invitation to eat Peruvian food at the Presidential House to help promote internal tourism.

Here we are, those of us who come home after a day's work and say, "I saw six dead bodies today," and those who want to change the subject. Those subject-changers charge thousands of dollars to solve a problem they neither understand nor try to understand. They're the same people who've never had trouble lifting their heads out of the volcano, those who realized much sooner than I have that Tegucigalpa is a city full of trees with red flowers and sunshine that breaks through the fog of the surrounding green hills. Because they can see more clearly looking towards the sky than they can with their eyes fixed at street level.

2

CRIME BEAT ROOKIE

The telephone rings one Saturday night, bringing news of death.

They just dropped two bodies, the policeman tells me over the phone. We'd asked him to show us the violence in San Pedro Sula, the so-called most violent city in the world. The cop—I can tell—feels useful lending a hand to a couple of international reporters.

I turn off the TV, put on my shoes, and tell the photographer about the call. As he routinely checks his memory cards and lenses, he phones for a taxi and checks the address with the receptionist. It's just another day for him. He's been covering this beat for more than a decade, since before I even started writing. He tells me to bring a phone charger, water, and some snacks to get us through the night—it could be a long one.

* * *

The first shots were fired through the front windshield. The victim's head reclines against the headrest. Inside the shattered skull there's something pink. Blood is spattered on the window, the steering wheel, the shirt.

The next victim is less bloody.

The bullet entered through the open window with nothing to interrupt its path. One shot is all it took—a little red dot at the temple. It's not as messy, but has left the body contorted, slumped to the side where it wanted to fall. The seatbelt is the only thing keeping the victim upright.

The bodies belong to the drivers of two mini-busses. This night, sweating as you can only sweat during Holy Week in the Caribbean, is my first night working the streets of Honduras.

They call it red journalism because of the blood. But the sparks that explode into the darkness are blue. The lights atop cop cars—rhythmic, hypnotic, as on American television shows—flood the scene like a spectacle for the faithful, those attending the nightly liturgy.

The police, four of them dropping grim-faced out of the bed of a pickup truck, look exhausted before they even begin their work. One of them makes a gesture with his rifle and, without even needing to issue an order, the crowd around the two mini-busses backs away. The officers wrap yellow tape around the scene. To get close enough to see, you elbow your way through the wall of crowding neighbors. A notepad or a camera is all the verification needed to let you scrutinize the corpses without raising eyebrows. The photographer doesn't waste time. He lifts the yellow tape, leans in, and shoots the victims again and again.

Lingering, I sit on a curb to smoke. In a little under an hour the scene has turned into a death carnival. Street-sellers jingle their cart-bells and onlookers gather around to buy candy, water, juice, and *baleadas*, Honduran-style tortilla sandwiches. The public eats, chats, loses enthusiasm. But almost nobody leaves. The television crews, completing the cast, move from one body to another. They get shots of the bodies, the curious spectators, the fat cop working the crowd. This is what they came for. Finally, someone drapes sheets over the bodies, and the local journalists turn off their cameras as if the show were over.

On that hot, viscous night in San Pedro Sula, there were eighteen murders. It's a city that averages fifteen homicides a day, and about 5,400 a year. In San Pedro Sula there are more violent deaths than in Baghdad or Kabul.

To write red journalism is to collect first-hand material from cadavers, to submerge yourself up to your eyeballs. Your Saturday nights will be dates with dead bodies and open notebooks. The challenge for the photographer is to capture the death scene without ruining the reader's breakfast the next morning; my challenge is to explain why it matters that these people are dying. No. That's too clichéd. To deliver to my editors a story that will justify their expenses. To find witnesses who will speak. To get them to talk, though talking puts them in danger. To give their personal details: full name, age, profession. To set up road signs on the map for whoever wants to find them, and charge them—with their lives—for speaking. Just basic professional standards.

I look around. The local journalists aren't asking questions. All they need is the number of bodies and the number of gunshots. They tend to avoid complication. And they help witnesses avoid complications. The script tells you to wait until the dust settles. I'm the kind of writer who always sticks close to the photographer. If he's going to linger at a scene, so am I. Minutes tick by. There, in plain view of the body, we talk about vacation plans, apartment rentals, sex, movies, our kids, Spain, Peru, the heat, the beach, prices for discount flights to Roatán Island—which is just half an hour from here. Another thirty minutes pass. Then an hour. An hour and a half before the forensic official comes to haul away the corpses.

This is the moment when they shine the lights again, when heads in the crowd turn to see: the unsavory moment when the attendants from the morgue have to pull the bodies out of the minivans and stuff them into plastic bags. For a crime photographer, these moments are like a landscape painter's sunset. We're sick. All of us. Those of us who think that our presence is justified because we're working; those who bring their kids to see the spectacle as if they were in their own living rooms watching a cheap movie. The bodies thunk out of their seats; the attendants heave them up again, trying not to drag them across the ground. I'll never understand why bodies always lose one or both shoes. The photographer catches a fresh portrait. Arms hanging like dead weight, a drooping head nodding goodbye, a puddle of blood seeping off the seat, advancing slowly towards the ground. News in this town lasts as long as the blood stays wet. Details harden quickly. *What*, *when*, *how*, and *who* turn into ends in themselves. The four basic questions of journalism gobbling up the fifth. The repetition blanks the *why*. There's talk, sure, but not about anything important.

* * *

As soon as they arrive, I spot them. On the street corner, a few steps removed from the circus surrounding the vans. They're not spectators. About a dozen men, a few women. They hug. Cry. Make phone calls. No cops or local journalists approach. Even if they did, they wouldn't want to talk to them. They're the victims. Those who know what happened. The people who can answer the *why* that nobody's asking.

I don't know where I find the will to overcome my shame, but I walk up to them. A few words of condolence and a short introduction identify me as a foreigner. The friends and family of the murdered drivers, angry and scared, want to step away and ask not to be identified before offering me any comment that might ease their rage. They're willing to talk only because I'm a foreigner. They think that whatever I write won't be read by anyone in town. But with the internet, that's unlikely.

Nobody provides their name. They have faces, clothes, stories, and fear, but they're missing names, which means what they tell me cannot be part of the story. They aren't the anonymous sources that will let an editor, in some office thousands of miles away, believe that through them the world can understand pain and truth. They can't help with my work; but they can help me.

They talk so that they won't be forgotten. But they don't denounce or accuse, nor do they provide details that could lead to the killers—and they know exactly who the killers are. They're not heroes; they don't want recognition, or fame. They don't even want to talk to me for longer than it takes to smoke a cigarette. They don't want to be known for running their tongues, only to have them cut out.

They start with the basic facts.

As they finished their last route of the day, the two drivers parked their vans next to each other to chat as their passengers disembarked. A group of men wielding pistols, their faces uncovered, stormed onto the scene and screamed at the passengers to hurry. The commuters ran, didn't look back, and the men executed the drivers.

Next comes the motive.

Each driver pays a fixed extortion fee of ten dollars per vehicle per week. People, including kids, are stationed throughout the city, notebooks in hand, to keep track of the busses, routes, fares, and average number of passengers. Occasionally, depending on how much business the drivers have, the gangs will increase their extortion fee. The collectors, who are always the same, collect openly from the drivers, even in the light of day.

The gangs select a driver responsible for putting the money in an envelope and waiting for a call to be given directions to the drop-off. Then the collector comes, on foot, motorcycle, or in a luxury truck, shakes the driver's hand, asks how business is going, and accepts payment.

But that morning, after following the payment ritual, somebody showed up to collect a second time. Explaining that they'd already paid, the driver realized that the first collector wasn't from the usual gang. The driver asked to talk to whoever was in charge to explain that somebody was robbing them, and he knew who.

But the collector didn't want to hear it—a thug who listens to reason won't incite fear. He told the driver that he was the one lying, and that someone would have to pay the price and be killed.

The driver started calling other drivers, warning anyone he saw back at the station, and doing what he could to avoid the inevitable. Those who got the warning burned through their contacts. Stop driving. Get out of your vans. They're going to kill. It's them. It's real. Urgent. Two of the drivers, used to this kind of thing, didn't pay much attention, and kept on driving. Losing a day's wages was more than they could afford. Now, they're dead.

The other drivers try to console themselves. It could have been worse. If they hadn't found those two, they might have gone to the bus station, where there were twenty of us.

All of those twenty drivers pay the owner a daily rate for use of the vehicles. Whether they find passengers or not. On top of that is the extortion fee. Thus, the fee that goes to the gang comes out of the drivers' pockets, not the business. The drivers don't want to talk to the police. They don't want to talk to the owner. It's their problem and they have to deal with it. What's the point of complaining and asking for help if nobody responds?

The owner's only concern when he shows up at the crime scene is for the other drivers to pull the bodies out of the vans, recover the collected fares, and do whatever they can to stop the police from taking the vehicles away as evidence. The drivers refuse.

As the owner approaches, the drivers lower their voices, and then go silent. As if in a play, the actors leave the stage, making room for the next act.

The owner, with his arms crossed over his chest, speaks loudly enough—he's nearly screaming—for everybody at the scene to hear. The same way the drivers talk about the gang, he talks about the authorities. Nobody is going to investigate, because whoever investigates is going to close down their little goldmine. These are his words. Some of the cops are in business with the gangs, and some of them have even left the force to start their own cells. It's true that none of the cops at the scene are asking any questions, or looking for witnesses, or conducting any sort of investigation. The officer closest to me stares ahead, without even blinking.

The night wears on. The victims' families have arrived, and I watch from afar. I feel like the old lady who watches you climb the staircase through a crack in her door. I keep on watching, but unlike the local journalists who snap and flash photos, I let the scene unfold in front of me without taking part.

A woman jumps out of a taxi. Like a well-rehearsed scene—everybody knowing their cue—the crowd stares at her idly. It's the wife of one of the drivers. She yells his name. The crowd, still gathered around the yellow tape, moves to give her space. The police officers know she's coming straight for the body. They should stop her. But they let her through, let her zip open the bag, let her hold and kiss the man's face one more time before, delicately, they pull her away, her face stained with blood. Two other women—sisters, or cousins, or maybe neighbors—take over from there. Now the widow will fall to the ground, cry out, and the women will pull her to her feet, console her, fanning her in front of the cameras and the crowds. It always goes like this, they tell me. And yet I still have trouble believing it.

A boy is behind the cluster of women. Nobody pays attention to him, and he's not crying. It's the dead man's son. In a matter of seconds he has grown up. I, however, do cry. I step away. Gain some distance. Turn my back. I let the dramatic tension drain away. I light a cigarette. Take a sip of juice. And I wait for the crowd to leave. It takes a long time.

Distancing myself from the crowd, however, has made me an easy target.

A group of teenage girls in tight t-shirts and short shorts detect a solitary, exotic foreigner who has infiltrated their world; they attack him with an arsenal of stares. I fail to understand their slang. They whisper and cackle to each other. One of them, full of energy and aplomb—also gorgeous— comes to ask me for a cigarette to verify the speculations, and to begin the questioning, the coyness, the seduction. I have no doubt that she's a minor. She asks for my number, the address of my hotel, and then tells me that we can go there as soon as I want. I don't give it to her. In Honduras, they call them prepaid women, or escort girls. I glance behind me, wondering if some overbearing cousin might be controlling things from across the street. I'm scared. I don't want to be the next corpse of the night, and in San Pedro Sula the nights are long.

The photographer and the taxi driver wouldn't let me forget, from my first until my last day as a correspondent in Honduras, about being taunted by the prepaid girl and her friends.

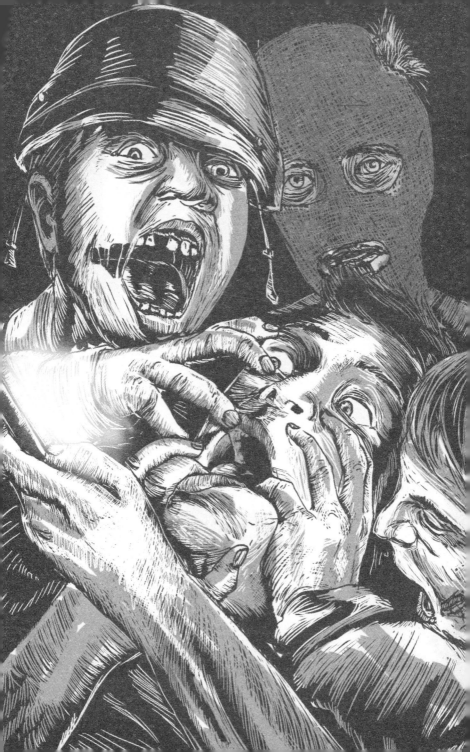

3

NIGHT OF THE CHEPOS

In Tegucigalpa there's nothing at all that could convince a responsible teenage boy to ditch his parents' home and brave the dangers of the night. Nothing at all except, of course, chasing a girl. Ebed Yanes, a studious middle-class fifteen-year-old, had been chatting with a girl on Facebook, and now he wanted to meet her in person. He ate dinner, helped his mom with some chores, said goodnight, and then went up to his room. "My parents are still awake," Ebed wrote to the girl that night from his bedroom. "I've got keys to the motorcycle. I'll shower and wait for them to go to sleep." Ebed never got to meet the girl.

Nobody else in the house realized that, around midnight, Ebed snuck down the stairs, got on his father's red motorcycle, and disappeared into the darkness. He took a few wrong turns, got lost, and then started getting scared. "I don't know what kind of hole you live in," he texted the girl. "I've been looking for you for forty-five minutes. I should probably get back home before I get caught by the chepos." Chepos, a

Honduran slang word for soldiers, was the last word he would write in his life. By 1:30 in the morning, in a dark and narrow alleyway, Ebed was lying dead on top of his dad's motorcycle, one bullet through his neck, two bullets in his back.

The Yanes family lives in one of the gated, high-security neighborhoods that abound on the outskirts of Tegucigalpa. Ebed's father, Wilfredo, a successful food distributor, welcomes me to their comfortable, two-story, middle-class home, which is furnished with the kind of banality that highlights an effort to maintain normalcy in the midst of utter chaos. We walk among old sofas, the walls punctuated by framed family portraits and diplomas. On the second floor there's a small TV room and three bedrooms. Next to the bedroom that will forevermore lie empty, Wilfredo, his wife (a university professor), and his oldest daughter (a medical student) share the few luxuries they allow themselves: a plasma television screen and an exercise machine so they can stay in shape without risking their lives out on the streets.

The family's tragedy began on Sunday morning. Wilfredo remembers waking up and finding that the red Toyota, which Ebed was supposed to have cleaned before church, was still dirty. It didn't worry him, though. His son and wife had gone over homework assignments together until late the night before, and there was nothing abnormal about his son avoiding his household chores. After eating breakfast, and repeatedly yelling that it was time to come down, Ebed's sister went upstairs to wake him. She found that his bed hadn't been slept in. Ebed's phone was off, and, checking the garage again, they realized that the motorcycle Wilfredo had recently bought to cut his commute time was missing. Wilfredo knew that his son was mischievous. He loved girls, and seemed to have a bit of an attention deficit disorder, but he never got into actual trouble; he usually obeyed his parents, he'd never been involved in anything serious, he didn't go out alone, and he didn't even know how to navigate the complicated system of collective taxis and busses that make up Honduras' public transportation system. When he went to his Taekwondo classes, his sister would drive him and wait for him out in the car, poring over her anatomy books. The night that Ebed was murdered in an alleyway was the first and last time in his life that he left the house without one of his family members.

Although Wilfredo had immediately sensed that something was wrong that morning—Honduran parents, bombarded by the violence surrounding them, panic when their kids get caught up in what is normally typical teenage behavior—he never imagined the worst. He started, naturally, by looking for him. The neighborhood security guard worried he'd be fired if he covered for Ebed, and admitted that the boy had left the neighborhood on a motorcycle after midnight the night before, and hadn't yet returned. But the guard had no reason to fear; neither Wilfredo nor his wife were vengeful types. They wanted to find their son, not point fingers, and they didn't think twice about the security guard. Wilfredo began whispering a mantra to himself: "We need to keep calm, but keep looking." They spent twelve long hours, running between the Criminal Investigation Unit, the Public Prosecutor's Office for Minors, and the children's hospital. They wanted to believe that he'd gotten into a motorcycle accident, or had stayed the night with some girl and that, any minute, he'd be back asking for forgiveness.

As if delaying news could change its course, it wasn't until late in the day that Wilfredo decided to go to the police department's homicide unit. Officials didn't know anything definitive there, either. They did, however, know of a red motorcycle that had showed up along with the corpse of an unidentified young man, killed by unknown suspects who fled without trace—an explanation repeatedly given by Honduran police to mask their incapacity, and unwillingness, to solve crimes.

"We have the motorcycle here. Do you want to see it?"

The family walked to the parking lot and, even from a distance, Wilfredo recognized his red motorcycle. He knew what it meant.

"Is it him?," his wife asked.

"Yes. It's him," Wilfredo responded; and then his wife fainted.

They went to the morgue. In silence the whole way. Wilfredo wanted to go in alone to identify the body. The process was quick and to the point. The morgue, as always at the weekends, was full. Ebed's body lay on the floor in a plastic bag. A bullet had shattered the jaw he still didn't have to shave. Wilfredo maintained composure. An official handed him a paper bag with his son's belongings: a BlackBerry full of text messages, a broken helmet, and a keychain. They were the keys to the house. That same night, during a vigil that lasted until dawn, Wilfredo made a promise to Ebed and a promise to his country. It was grandiloquent. Since his son's death, that's how Wilfredo is. And it's his right. With each word, each gesture, his obsession in keeping all newspaper clippings of his son's case, his organizing a notebook filled with the appointments made with prosecutors, journalists, and politicians he's trying to influence. But besides being an orderly person, he's also a profoundly religious person, and refuses to allow a crime like the one committed against his son to be judged only in heaven, because God, as he told me, will judge you for what you do on earth. That very day of the funeral he decided to start investigating. He promised himself that his son wouldn't be reduced to yet another statistic. He couldn't believe what the police had told him. His son—the victim of a random murder in the street? He just didn't believe it. From the day of the funeral, before he was even buried, he started dealing with his pain by searching for the truth. And he found it.

Wilfredo needed to shower and change before the funeral. He also wanted to be alone to think. But on the way home he realized he couldn't even wait until his son was in the ground to start his investigation. He made a couple of detours before grabbing that shower and change of clothes. The first stop was a police station a little more than a hundred meters from where his son's body had turned up. "Yeah, we heard shots," an officer told him. "But we didn't go outside. We were scared." Wilfredo didn't blame them. He wasn't very critical of the government, or the police. Realizing they weren't able to fulfill even their basic duties, he didn't have anything else to discuss with them. He was looking for information and gained nothing from excuses, deflections, or even condolences. Above all, he was a practical man. His second stop that morning was the alleyway where his son had been killed. Maybe somebody had seen or heard something. He realized it was likely nobody would want to talk even if they had seen something, but he needed to try, and he would not be disappointed. It turned out that people can't resist a father broken by pain; plus, he wasn't a cop, he was a neighbor. He was one of them, he was relatable, and he was able to discover what a whole army of detectives never could have discovered.

One neighbor told him she heard what sounded like rifle shots in the middle of the night, but was scared to peek out, but then mentioned some others who might have risked a glance. One neighbor, brave enough to look through the curtains, was also willing to talk: he'd seen a group of seven or eight men in uniform approach a body splayed out on top of a motorcycle, turn the body over with their guns, gather up the shells, and then jump into a double-cabin four-by-four pickup truck. According to the witness, the uniformed men returned to the scene a few minutes later to do another inspection, this time with flashlights, making sure that no evidence had been left behind. But they were too hasty. In every cover-up, if someone looks hard enough, there's always a trail to be found. The next morning, at dawn, the witness picked up a few shells the men had missed in the darkness and gave them to Wilfredo. Those shells—on which were written the name and number "*Aguila 223*"—Wilfredo carried with him in a plastic bag to his son's funeral.

Wilfredo remembers tossing dirt over his son's coffin with one hand, while the other gripped the bullet shells in his pocket. He couldn't get the idea out of his head that it wasn't some random shooter in the street but the Honduran Army that had senselessly killed his son.

The Monday after the funeral, Wilfredo sought advice from Julieta Castellanos, the dean of the National Autonomous University of Honduras, whose son was shot dead by police at a checkpoint in 2011, and who has since become a vocal critic of the impunity of the Honduran security forces. Despite the fact that the police who killed her son escaped, Castellanos has stood as an example to parents like Wilfredo to look beyond the meager investigations of impotent state forces. People at the university recommended that Wilfredo wait before bringing charges, that he not speak to the media, that discretion is best, and that he go to the Human Rights Division of the Public Prosecutor's Office and tell them everything he knows—that the investigators would need all the help they could get. The week of his son's funeral, on a Thursday, Wilfredo and his wife became detectives. They started spending their insomniac nights exhausting their pain in the streets, searching for an Army pickup truck similar to the one the witness had described. They found nothing. But they looked, and looked, and kept looking. Exactly a week after the murder, the following Saturday at midnight, they drove past a military checkpoint, not far from where their son was murdered. Wilfredo spotted a truck, a Ford F350 Super Duty, which looked almost like a tank. These kinds of trucks are rare in Tegucigalpa. Wilfredo asked his wife to slow down so he could take a picture through the window. The flash, however, alerted the soldiers, and they stopped the car. They surrounded Wilfredo and his wife, took their camera, and began questioning them. Wilfredo told them they were on their way home to eat, and that he liked to take pictures of rare vehicles. It worked. He and the soldiers talked about the size of the motor and the sticker price of the latest model, not of murdered children. The soldiers let them go. They didn't see any reason to suspect a middle-class married couple on their way home for supper.

Back home, still trembling, Wilfredo copied the photos onto a USB and then erased them from his camera. He was scared that someone would come into his house at night and steal the camera. He already had the bullet casings, and now he had photographs of a vehicle that matched the witness description, as well as the location of a checkpoint that accorded with events he still couldn't bear to play out in his head. That Monday, just eight days after his son's murder, Wilfredo went to the Human Rights Division and presented all the evidence he'd uncovered.

Afterwards, Wilfredo wasn't ready to sit at home and wait—he knew he might very well wait forever. Instead, following advice, he went to the office of Chief Prosecutor German Enamorado, and he told him that he was in a hurry and needed information. And he insisted. All day, three days in a row, he insisted. Enamorado later told me he was impressed by Wilfredo's persistence. If it was true that a group of soldiers had murdered a young kid, then they had a horrific crime on their hands. For a man so accustomed to dealing with the abuse of authority, and the political impossibility of pursuing certain crimes, he barely had enough tools to actually do his job. Though, of course, he still had to put on enough of a show to make it seem as if he was following leads. He assigned an officer and a prosecutor to the case. But they didn't even have a vehicle to begin their investigation. The Prosecutor's Office is a place so inundated by files that officers are nearly drowning in paperwork. About 600 open cases for each officer overwhelms even the best intentions. On top of all the cases, a half-dozen prosecutors share just a single vehicle, with a meager stipend for gas. That Wilfredo offered to act as chauffeur, day after day, without complaint, along with his pleasant attitude and treating prosecutors to coffee, won their respect and was key to advancing the case. He generated empathy in the office, which he saw as going above and beyond what was expected in a country where all factors push officials towards shirking responsibility. Without the initiative, the capacity, the time, and the well-organized resources that Wilfredo brought to the office—where a full tank of gas was considered a luxury—the investigators would not have been able to do a thing.

Days later Wilfredo got a call from one of the prosecutors asking for a ride to start following some leads. With Wilfredo at the wheel, the first stop was the military barracks where, they assumed, they would find paperwork related to the night in question. Instead, they hit a wall. They had to cross the city multiple times, from one station to another, until finally someone told them that any request for paperwork needed to be written out and addressed to the proper authority. With persistence, much difficulty, and an order signed by a lead prosecutor, they finally got the document they were looking for. Signed by the official running the checkpoint on the night Ebed was assassinated, the document described a motorcyclist shooting at soldiers manning the checkpoint.

It went on to say that the soldiers chased after him, but that the motorcyclist was able to get away. This was only the first of the military's lies. A lie that sounded a lot like other lies; lies that had come before and would come later. But there was also an unexpected lead—the kind of detail that makes a particular story gain popular interest, a few gunshots calling into question an entire political stance. The soldiers that chased and killed Ebed were part of the Army's First Battalion of Special Forces. The battalion had received training from the United States, and had permission to run joint operations with the US military. In other words, they were the most highly trained and elite soldiers in Honduras, they had foreign assistance, and Wilfredo was convinced that they were the ones who'd killed his son.

The more details he uncovered, the more furious he became. Although I never saw him more than rightfully indignant, humble, and thankful to each person he asked for help, he was simmering beneath the surface. Without expressing it physically, or even through his words, and despite his earnest face and learned mannerisms, his eyeglasses and ironed shirts, he was driven by rage. His fury didn't express itself physically, but in the persistence and clarity of his ideas. For Wilfredo, the laws are firm, and should hold up to people's demands. History books, reports from international nonprofits, and even journalists use ready-made catchphrases and generalizations that allow us to feel that we can understand the situation of Honduras and other Central American countries in a thousand words. We write of the arrival of democracy in the region, of civil government, of the Army's loss of influence. Of the passage of constitutions, of codes of conduct that bring to an end, theoretically, prior codes of conduct. Of foreign military assistance that doesn't kill, but stops the killing and establishes the rule of law. And some citizens believe this to be true. Wilfredo knows, because the prosecutor explained it to him, after consulting the Army's code of conduct, that soldiers cannot fire their weapons unless they are confronted with a direct and lethal threat. That there are protocols: stop, identify, warn, detain—a whole series of steps that should be taken before firing, unless it is in self-defense. That is how democracy is supposed to work. Any other course of action, outside of the protocol, is illegal. His son was armed with nothing but a cellphone. Now that Wilfredo had spotlighted high-profile players, the case flooded the press, and powerful figures started to elaborate the lies. Democracy was failing him—day by day, lie by lie—as it had failed so many other victims and their families.

The military now claimed that Ebed must have been "up to something." The state was giving more credibility to the Army, in charge of protecting the homeland, than one civilian victim. They blasted the possibility that the boy was a gang member—though, given the twenty homicides a day, that was hard to verify. Commander of the Honduran Army,

René Osorio, publicly declared that Ebed declined to stop at a military checkpoint and had deserved what happened to him. His exact words: "Logically, when a criminal comes to a checkpoint and does not stop, it's because he's doing something illegal." When the prosecutors questioned the soldiers who rode in the Ford truck that night, none of them claimed to have remembered a motorcycle, or even having driven the truck at all, and they certainly didn't remember having fired their weapons without lawful reason.

One of the soldiers, seeing his name in the press and realizing the savagery he was implicated in, took an unexpected turn—as unexpected, perhaps, as someone overcoming their fear after witnessing a shooting through their living-room curtains and then slipping into the street to collect bullet shells, or as unexpected as Wilfredo and his wife going out to spy on the checkpoint. He decided to speak out, to make a dignified exit, or at least to strategize a self-defense that was not in line with his superiors, something that the prosecutors could later latch onto in their investigation.

Shortly after the interrogation, one of the soldiers called his own mother and told her a different version of what had happened to Ebed. He told her he'd been ordered to lie. His mother then called a lawyer who explained that it was better to be a protected witness to the prosecution than be accused of murder. The soldier talked with other soldiers, and the next day, starting to feel nervous, a few more soldiers presented themselves at the Public Prosecutor's Office to tell their version of the story. The kid, they said, didn't stop at the checkpoint. He accelerated and motored right through it. They shot at him. He didn't stop. They chased him in their beast of a truck, the Ford F350 Super Duty, tearing through the night. The kid didn't have a chance. Desperate, he turned into a dead-end alleyway. The Ford blocked off the entrance and Second Lieutenant Sierra, who was in charge that night, started firing without even getting down from the truck. Following orders, two other soldiers started shooting. It all happened quickly, in the darkness. The soldiers—practically kids themselves, not one of them older than twenty-two—found themselves looking at a dead body. The kid on the motorcycle was dead, and they couldn't forget it.

Despite the rampant impunity that dominates Honduras, the soldiers were scared. Arguments and blame sprouted at the foot of Ebed's body. The common response (demanded by the hierarchy) was to cover for each other: all were implicated, so everyone had everyone's back. First, they swept the crime scene; only then did the second lieutenant report to his boss, Colonel Juan Girón, who ran the checkpoint. According to testimony gathered by the prosecutors, "[Juan Girón] told us what we were supposed to say ... that we weren't supposed to talk, especially not to the police, about what had happened." Another officer swapped out the guns (an M16, a Beretta, a Remington, and an R15) so that the ballistic tests wouldn't match up. A prosecutor had to repeatedly ask the minister of defense, Marlon Pascua, to hand over the weapons; Pascua did all he could to block the request.

Wilfredo was horrified. "They used my son as target practice." Prosecutor Enamorado explained that the soldiers would have been right to pursue Ebed, try to detain him by forming obstacles in the road, or even shoot into the air. But they absolutely should not have fired at a fleeing suspect who presented no threat. "Their actions were despicable," he said. "The law is clear on this. Ebed should not be dead."

What happened next was a miracle. Seventeen days after opening the case, thanks to Wilfredo's insistence, as well as the help he offered the Public Prosecutor's Office, and after the testimonies of some of the conscience-stricken soldiers, the three soldiers who shot at Ebed were arrested. Eliezer Rodríguez, the 22-year-old soldier who fired the fatal shot, was accused of murder and put in jail. The other two, including Second Lieutenant Sierra, who fired the first shots, were only accused of attempted cover-up and of acting in violation of their duties. They were both reassigned and waited for their trials as free men.

In some respects, Wilfredo had received justice. The crimes were made public, the Public Prosecutor's Office had brought charges against the man who killed his son, who was now locked up in a military prison. It was more justice than is usually found in Honduras. But, of course, he wasn't satisfied.

He would never be satisfied. In the end, the soldiers were following orders, and Wilfredo wasn't okay with the fact that a single soldier should take all the blame. And even that was uncertain; Rodriguez could very well be found innocent. In the Army, as we've learned from Hollywood movies, there's always the push to climb the ladder of rank. It's a ladder shrouded in fog, the top of which is almost impossible to see. Of course there were other guilty parties to Ebed's murder. Beyond the soldiers who fired the shots, there was Colonel Juan Girón who ordered his subordinates to lie; Colonel Reynel Funes, who swapped out the weapons to muddle the ballistic tests; Colonel Jesús Mármol, in charge of overseeing Operation Lightning, which has kept Tegucigalpa on an Army-imposed lockdown since the 2009 coup d'état, and who said that he'd never been informed of the murder, despite the fact that his subordinates claim otherwise.

The Army maintains that none of the officers committed misconduct. "All that about the lies and the swapping out of weapons is pure fiction," I was told by yet another colonel, the Armed Forces spokesperson Jeremías Arévalo. "We've cooperated with the prosecutors in everything since day one." Unsatisfied with the lie, he continued: "For us, the case is closed. We are a responsible branch of the military, and we are against impunity."

But Wilfredo wasn't satisfied. Months later, he was able to convince the Public Prosecutor's Office to investigate the role of the officers up the chain of command, and seek to discover what happened with the weapons used in the murder. In order to get their contradictions on record, the prosecutor called the colonels to testify.

The case even made news in the US, and not just in relation to the fact that the military equipment used to commit the crime came from the US. Reynel Funes, the colonel who supposedly ordered the gun swap, was working under US government approval. Like many high-ranking officers in the Honduran military, Reynel attended California's Naval Postgraduate School on scholarship in 2006, where he graduated with a Master's degree in Defense Analysis. He'd also previously studied at the School of the Americas (now known as the Western Hemisphere Institute for Security Cooperation) in Fort Benning, Georgia. It's not hard to think back to those US-backed Central American counterinsurgent armies of the 1980s, and see that, despite the arrival of democracy, not much has changed. Or that the more the United States meddles, the more it insists on trying to help countries which, just maybe, don't want to be helped, the more its hands come away bloody.

As of now, two years later, there haven't been any other breakthroughs in the case. Ebed's murder reached the international press. Television crews came. They interviewed Wilfredo and the prosecutors, who repeated the story again and again. The world knows what happened, but the guilty parties have yet to be sentenced. They haven't even been tried in court. And there's a good chance they never will be. A low-ranking officer, the one who fired the lethal shot, will stay in jail for a time, but after he's served his preventive sentence, he will go free. Probably, nobody else will face charges. In Honduras, cases die in their folders. The prosecutors assigned to the case have moved on. In Honduras, the turnover of prosecutors is one of the key reasons so few cases are actually heard at trial. Wilfredo knows it's difficult to achieve justice, he knows it was always unlikely that the case would actually go to trial, knows that his country wouldn't be able to shrug off decades of corruption and incompetency, knows that his neighbors still can't walk the streets at night and not feel afraid, knows that other fathers can't let their sons go for walks in the park or test the limits of their freedom without fearing for their lives, knows that it's impossible for Ebed to come back to him; and he also knows that it is possible that, in seeking justice, he himself could be killed.

4

DEATH OF A TAXI DRIVER

Willing to do anything to avoid covering the election, photographer Moisés Castillo and I were even willing to exhume corpses. Fifteen years had passed since Hurricane Mitch flooded the Choluteca River, destroying much of the city's downtown area. We were waiting for the ever-punctual Mairena to pick us up and drive us around the trash dump that the Choluteca turns into as it rolls through downtown. We thought we could get a feel for the area by spending some time with a group of men who work sifting sand out of the river to sell to construction companies. The rumor in Tegucigalpa is that any pick or shovel digging into the banks of the Choluteca will inevitably turn up human remains: the bones of thousands of people devoured by the river during the 1998 hurricane, which greatly added to the city's list of disappeared persons. Thousands of bodies that no one had the capacity to count or the will to find. The center of Tegucigalpa is a hulking, unsealed mass grave.

One of many journalistic vices is to look for metaphors in landscape.

* * *

Just as we were complaining about Mairena being late, a friend of his, Benjamín Álvarez Moncada, a sixty-eight-year-old taxi driver known as Don Mincho, sat waiting behind the wheel of a taxi for his turn to pick up the next client. He was parked behind the church on Los Dolores, a bustling market street in the middle of the city that was covered curb to curb in campaign ads for the upcoming November election. Don Mincho sat beneath the gaze of two presidential candidates, Xiomara Castro and Juan Orlando Hernández, both of whom wanted his vote. Maybe Don Mincho momentarily fixed his eyes on the nationalist candidate Juan Orlando Hernández, only to laugh at his campaign motto: "I'll do whatever it takes to improve law and order." Maybe campaign ads are rendered invisible to those who have no choice but to work beyond retirement in order to pay for their wife's prescriptions, the bills, the rent, car maintenance. Maybe campaign ads are an insult to the intelligence and dignity of any Honduran taxi driver.

Four in the afternoon—white-collar workers heading home, and taxi drivers starting their long evening shift. But the person who slowly inched up the right side of Don Mincho's car was not a client, but a fifteen-year-old hitman who fired three shots.

One in the temple.

Another through the ear.

The last in the neck.

That's why Mairena was late to pick us up. Not because of the traffic, but because his friend had been murdered.

When I got a call about the crime, Mairena wanted his journalist friends, just this once, to offer their services to him. He thought the death of Don Mincho had to be told. He thought that, in the end, he could just as easily have been the one murdered. He thought that driving journalists from one side of the city to the other should have some payoff. He thought of that lie ("we work so that the world will know") we had expounded to him so many times over beers after a day in the field. But this afternoon, to our pretentious proclamation, he countered with a succinct, "They've killed Don Mincho. Now go do your job."

We never did get to work on our sand-sifting story. We got sucked, once again, into the crime beat.

* * *

In a city that lacks organized public transportation and is built over steep and rugged slopes, many of the seventy-two legal taxi stations work with fixed routes and collective pick-up systems. Taxis—parked on the streets and waiting in line until they fill up with four passengers—offer the only mode of transportation for those who can't afford their own car. Passengers typically pay ten lempiras (less than fifty cents) for the trip. A taxi driver considers himself lucky if he's made 500 lempiras in a day (twenty-one dollars) after paying for gas, and, in most cases, a daily car rental, which is usually about twenty dollars a day. This is how drivers make a living, and this is how folks in the capital get to where they need to go.

In Tegucigalpa in 2012, thirty-three taxi drivers were murdered. That translates into a murdered cabbie every eleven days in a city half the size of Barcelona. Forty-one were murdered in 2013, and in 2014 the figure rose to sixty. This story isn't new. In fact, it's common: it's the story I know best, the story that gets told again and again. It has become an anecdote. And this time—because it's what Mairena demanded of us—we were the ones who had to tell the story.

As night began falling over the shattered city, the taxi drivers' first reaction that evening was—spontaneously, and without clear objective—to block traffic with their cars. "Stop!" screamed one driver. "Drop your passengers off. Let them walk home." No one answered. They didn't argue, they didn't object. Neither the drivers nor their passengers got upset. It was a process of collective healing. Everyone understood each other, everyone was in agreement. Everybody wants to go home at the end of the day. And yet no one knew what it meant for traffic to stop there, what the point was. Some followed directions and joined the improvised assembly without knowing what to say, or how to go beyond offering a general condolence. An assembly of losers without a leader, without speeches to applaud. Without asking for permission, and without going through any agenda items, they simply dispersed. This time, after acknowledging what had happened, everyone kept on working, kept their mouths shut, and not a single complaint was heard, not even from those at the front of the march. In reality, everyone knew that the passengers couldn't protest all the way home. Not at night. It would be too dangerous. They all shared the fear of extortion, they were all exhausted, and they all—filled with dismay and jumbled emotions—had their own personal problems. They were all in the same situation. No one offered a solution. There wasn't even anyone to confront.

Drivers watch out for each other as best they can. There are other ways to react when someone is killed, and they know them well. Mairena confesses that they've been through this before. All of them know of taxi drivers who, sick of paying up, decided they could only pay their extortionists with a taste of their own medicine. An unpaid bill can kill you in such a lawless city. If someone charges you 50,000 lempiras (about $2,100) to work, promising to kill you if you don't pay, you can solve the problem by finding someone to kill that person for 30,000 lempiras—as countless people have explained to me. But that won't work this time. It takes more than guts. These workers prefer not to descend into savagery.

Every Saturday for six years this taxi guild puts 5,500 lempiras (about $230) in an envelope and gives it to a child without so much as saying a word. Every taxi driver adds 150 lempiras to the envelope. Two weeks ago, a telephone call came through: a voice demanding 20,000 lempiras as a Christmas bonus. They didn't pay up. They said they couldn't. "They're playing with the hunger of our families," the bravest driver of the group told me. "I made a report," he added, "I testified with my face covered in a hood so that no one would recognize me." Now he feels guilty because he thinks his report may be responsible for his co-worker's murder. They had been warned. "On Thursday, that same kid came to the taxi station and put a gun to another driver's temple. He froze, and the kid didn't shoot. The driver locked himself in his house, turned off his cellphone, and said he wouldn't talk to anyone." His biggest weakness was his routine. "They get kids to study the numbers of each cab, the frequency of their trips, their schedules, where we live. With that, we can't escape. We're trapped. We're easy prey. Don Mincho was murdered because he was first in line. They weren't against him in particular. They were targeting the collective, not the person. If we go back, another one of us will fall tomorrow."

The next day, the doors to a church—a half-built shed— opened to a crowd of neighbors waiting in silence. While the drivers laid the coffin in a car bound for the cemetery, the National Party distributed discount cards from a small tent to the residents of the La Cachureca neighborhood. The presidential candidate Juan Orlando Hernández, defender of iron-fist policies, the one who peered down from his campaign poster as Don Mincho was shot, was giving away free t-shirts and registering voters. At least he had the decency to turn off the music that he usually blares throughout the neighborhood while he campaigns.

After the religious ceremony, someone opened the coffin and, standing in line to view, hug, and kiss the body, the drivers wept—all of them—sharing stories of the last time they'd been with their colleague and friend. Moisés, the photographer, had the tact not to take any pictures, not wanting to identify any of the drivers with an image and caption that could blast through the internet. It'd be even worse if that face were followed by an article critiquing the police force or a gang. On the drive back home while trying to make a plan for tomorrow, one of the drivers explained: "There are only two options: pay the war tax or migrate to the US."

* * *

The day after the murder, as night fell once again, the taxi station Los Dolores-El Bosque sat empty; the drivers, after losing a day of work, had to ask each other for loans. Two, three days later, the situation grew worse. Some of them, overtaken by a temporary feeling of intimacy as they recounted their problems to me, so that I could do my job—as Mairena

ALBERTO ARCE

had exhorted me to do—asked me for money, because they
couldn't go back to their jobs before paying off the extortion
fee they owed. It seemed a reasonable exchange. Days passed
with more of the same. I'd ask them questions, and they would
explain to me different possible solutions, complaining of
how fragmented they felt and recounting their arguments
with each other until, finally, they were able to scrape together
the 20,000 lempiras their extortionists demanded, and were
finally able to get back to work. How did they manage it, in
the end? Someone gave them a loan at a forty percent interest
rate so that they'd be able to pay up, so that they'd be able to
go back to their salary of 160 lempiras a day.

Among the drivers once again putting their necks on the
line was Mincho's grandson, Daniel, who now sat behind
the same wheel his grandfather had turned. Now he was
responsible for scraping together the money for the same
prescription medicine that had forced his grandfather to work
beyond retirement. After seeing the new generation take the
reins, and the cycle completed, my relationship to the story
gradually faded. I limited myself to greeting Daniel with
only two honks of the horn and a wave out the window of
Mairena's taxi whenever we crossed paths. In a week's time, I
stopped asking questions, sick of hearing answers that would
never lead anywhere.

Two months later there was news. The treasurer of the taxi
guild of Los Dolores, the one who was in charge of collecting

money every week from his co-workers and putting it in an envelope for the extortionists, the same who had worked with the taxi guild for years, and who everyone knew since he was a kid and who had cried as much as anyone else at Mincho's funeral, was arrested by the newly created National Anti-extortion Force while carrying an inexplicably large amount of money. He was the one who had extorted his colleagues. No one was surprised. It was hardly news. The world learning that Henry—a taxi driver under the constant threat of death—had begun extorting his colleagues would do nothing to fix the situation, and would do nothing to help Mairena, and nothing at all to help Mincho's grandson.

5

FOUR BOARDS
STRAPPED TO THE BACK

Edwin Mejía didn't want to work that morning. The seventy-five dollars he'd landed the day before by stealing a motorcycle with his friend was a fortune compared to the four dollars a day he typically pulled in selling his mother's tortillas door to door. The teenager, just turned fifteen, was still lingering in his wooden one-room house, stretched out on the bed he shared with his brothers, when he told his partner-in-crime, Eduardo Aguilar, who'd come looking for him to go hit the streets, that he just wasn't in the mood. "Come on, let's go, we gotta go," insisted Eduardo, who'd also just turned fifteen. Eduardo was planning to buy a phone with yesterday's money. If he was as lucky today, he'd be able to buy himself a pair of white Nikes—a must-have for members of the Barrio 18 (18th Street) gang. Edwin caved. They drank a coffee before leaving the wooden hilltop house and heading to Tegucigalpa. It was almost lunchtime. They decided to stick to the same plan as yesterday: when they found their victim Eduardo would threaten him, and then together they would ride off on the stolen motorcycle. It would be a cinch: Edwin driving, with Eduardo riding on the back.

Several kilometers away, in the center of Tegucigalpa, traffic officer Santos Arita started his twelve-hour workday. At forty-two years old, he'd spent most of his life regulating traffic in the towns and villages of northern Honduras. Arita had been relocated to Tegucigalpa two months before, and he anxiously awaited a change in luck that would let him go home. He missed his family. He wasn't happy where they'd stationed him, in the capital. Three armed teenagers had already assaulted him once on a bus. He was afraid of working the streets in a city where people were willing to kill for anything. He'd told all this to his wife and kids; but no one had asked him if he was in the mood to work that day.

According to a law meant to lower the murder rate, it's illegal for two men to ride a motorcycle together. Crime is easy in this country, and a motorcycle makes for a fast escape. That's why, in theory, and only in theory, motorcycles are kept under close watch. The boys, who were well aware of this law, couldn't care less as they made their way downtown. They were also aware that virtually no one was ever caught. It was strange how in one of the poorest and most chaotic cities in the continent, where the law is seldom followed, what fated these two fledgling gang members to cross paths with a poor traffic officer was the fact that they had heeded a red light.

Shortly after stealing the motorcycle, they stopped at a traffic light in front of one of the largest banks in Honduras. They didn't see that just behind them Officer Arita was helping a woman, who held a parasol to protect her from the sun, cross the street. No one would have guessed that this would be his only and last good deed of the day. The very last of his life. No one trusts the police in Honduras, or thinks anything good of them. Officer Arita could have done what most officers do, could have pretended not to see, could have looked the other way, and let the boys go. But Arita wanted to do his job.

What happened that afternoon at the traffic light was recorded on a security camera. When Arita saw the two boys on the bike, he left the woman with the parasol and ran after them. He grabbed the keys of the motorcycle and began to struggle with Eduardo, who reached for his gun and fired two times, missing his target. Edwin lurked just above the fight, trying to help his partner. In the confusion, he came away with the gun. That was when Arita lost his balance and fell to the ground. As he tried to get back on his feet, Edwin shot him, at close range, twice in the head. He died instantly. Calmly, Eduardo picked up the keys from the ground, waited for Eduardo to get back on the motorcycle, and sped away. The whole drama lasted only forty-two seconds.

The passing drivers kept driving, trying to outrun their fear. No one intervened.

The teenagers fled the scene on their motorcycle before abandoning it and continuing on foot down the middle of a five-lane avenue. They passed in front of the Clarion hotel, a Burger King, and a McDonald's. They tried to take over a running bus, aiming their gun at the driver, who sped off. A pair of armed kids in plain daylight wasn't something that surprised people in the center of Tegucigalpa. We've all seen it. To stay out of trouble, you only have to lock your car doors, hit the gas and pass the scene without gawking. Typically, they would have escaped. But they had killed a police officer and this time other officers took action. A police murderer shouldn't go unpunished, not if it can be helped. Two officers gave chase, arrested the boys, and brought them to a station parking lot next to the Marriot Hotel, which is on the same block as the Presidential Palace, one of the most well-guarded buildings in the country. From that moment on, the police gave no further explanations. They didn't let anyone view the security camera footage of the arrest, though footage of the murder was leaked to the press.

* * *

"They started beating us on our arms and feet. They would hit my head with the barrel of a gun, and they kept saying they were going to kills us," Edwin told me a few weeks later as he was sitting in the jail's courtyard. Several patrol officers and even a group of soldiers joined in the beating. When the police noticed that too many people were watching, they took the kids, now badly injured, to Tegucigalpa's central police transit center. There, in an open-air parking lot, the beating continued for three hours. "One guy showed up who would grab me by the hair and pin me down so that another one could kick and punch me," Edwin remembers. They'd laugh, insult, and threaten the boys while other agents took pictures with their phones.

Eduardo was taken to Hospital Escuela, where he died four hours later. The autopsy showed that the cause of death was more than twenty hits to the base of the cranium with a blunt object, probably a gun. Edwin survived by pure accident, a mistake. They were after him. He was the one who'd fired the mortal shots.

According to prosecutor Alexis Santos, the investigator for the case, the boys were not legally detained, something to alarm any prosecutor. It wasn't an arrest, but a public lynching, a torture session. For Santos, the charges against the officers were obvious: illegal detention, torture with the result of death, neglect of an officer's duties, and criminal cover-up. He thinks Eduardo's death was part of a policy of "social cleansing" that would not be possible without the collaboration—of either enthusiasm or omission—from the local press. No government official or police officer was asked to comment, defend, or explain themselves, because no journalist asked them to.

A local newspaper, *La Tribuna*, published pictures of the kids in police detention. The pictures showed Eduardo on the floor without a shirt, unconscious and covered in blood. Edwin was shown against a wall, handcuffed and also covered in blood, his eyes swollen.

Publishing these pictures was in no way exceptional. It's common for images of tortured or killed victims to wind up on the cellphones of local photographers. The photographer who receives this kind of picture knows who sent it, he comments on it through WhatsApp, and even publishes it. But in cases like this, the informant is not acting as a journalist, he doesn't investigate the actions captured in the photograph, he doesn't criticize, he doesn't question, he doesn't waste time grappling with theories on the protocols of a legal detention. Instead, in a case like this, he turns the published picture into an example.

Journalists who publish these pictures wouldn't even think to collaborate with the Public Prosecutor's Office. They say they're afraid. But it's not true, they're not afraid to collude with their police officer friends. The journalists and cops feed off each other. I've gotten to know this breed of journalist: I'm convinced they believe the police are in the right. Their bosses think this way, the big editors of the major Honduran outlets, and even the majority of readers think this way—not only do they approve of this violence, but they actively seek more blood. The epidemic of crimes taking over the country has given rise to a culture that believes in an eye for an eye, a tooth for a tooth. "They're too dangerous to be allowed to live, people like that should die," a reader commented when these pictures were published. "Too bad they didn't kill the other one, I hope that they kill and rape him in Tamara [Prison]," another commenter hoped. "One less rat on earth," a third added cheerfully.

The prosecutor summarized the situation in one sentence: "People ask themselves what more could be investigated when we know he was the one who killed the police officer." But Santos, unlike the press, does investigate, though he doesn't think he'll find the proof necessary to incriminate the police. When he asked for the names of the officers involved in the lynching, he was given a list of all the transit officers working that day, even the ones who worked many kilometers away. More than a hundred names in all. On top of that, not one officer was asked to testify. The prosecutor isn't given an assistant or a car, not even a motorcycle to use to investigate a case. There's no one to protect him when he faces the alleged murderers in police uniform. These are the same officers who could even pay him a surprise visit.

* * *

After the police murder, one family in Ocotepeque was left broken and impoverished. I met with them in a hotel in the city, some eight hours from the capital, weeks after the murder.

Arita's partner, twenty-eight-year-old Suyapa Pineda, came with her three kids: fourteen-year-old Joaquín, eleven-year-old Jairo, and six-year-old Marjorie. "My dad's a policeman, but he was assaulted," Marjorie said—many months later she still believed her dad was away working, and would soon return for a visit. The kids were hungry. Or that's what they told me. After filling their bellies, they took me to their house. Honduran police officers, often accused of corruption or murder, live in miserable conditions. Not so different from their murderers. When I stepped into their house, I noticed how similar it was to any gangster's house. Built of clay, with a cement floor, a precarious and leaky tin roof, and with two of its four walls made of wooden planks, you could barely even call it a room. "When you shut the door, the whole house shakes," said the oldest son, Joaquín. The only furniture is two beds, a rickety couch, a pair of tables, and a lamp. There is no running water, and the kitchen is a wood stove. "The kids pick up in the morning and that's where I cook," said Suyapa. "Two days before they killed him, he went to Tegucigalpa with 200 lempiras and leaving 200 more with us. Santos would spend twelve hours without eating or drinking, standing in traffic under the sun, and, when he couldn't handle it anymore, he'd have to ask someone for a few lempiras so that he could eat a tortilla and have a little water," Suyapa explained, justifying police officers forced to ask for small bribes in exchange for not giving out a ticket at a traffic stop.

"After they killed him, I went to Tegucigalpa and saw the room where he used to live. A terrible box, too cold and too hot, where everyone sleeps together, with the door open, without any privacy. They bathe in a barrel of water. They don't even get food. Everyone says that police steal and kill. But police who steal and kill don't live in a wooden box or get home by thumbing for rides. Most of them are dying of hunger, and are harmless. One does something bad, and everyone has to pay for it. If you haven't seen the reality of a police officer, you have no right to judge."

Only Joaquín, who stopped going to school to help his family by selling paintings (and earning about five dollars a day) has seen the video of his father's murder. "It was good for me to see it. My dad was a hero. Now I know. My dad was a good policeman. He was an honest policeman. At school they told me my dad was killed because he tried to extort people. I had to beat the kid who said that." Despite what he's seen, or perhaps because of what he's seen, Joaquín wants to be a police officer. "My dad always told me that I should be a police chief or a general."

On our way to her house from the hotel, and without her kids around her, Suyapa told me stories of Arita. Just like Joaquín and her other children, she called him "Dad."

"I'm not losing a husband. I'm losing a father," she said.

"How's that?"

"He picked me up off the street when I was eleven years

old and he raised me like he was my dad. He raised me like his own daughter, both me and the kids he gave me. I loved him like a father. I didn't like giving him children very much, but he took good care of me."

* * *

In the juvenile detention center of Tegucigalpa, Edwin is awaiting trial. Sitting on a chair in the prison courtyard, he seems more like a lost child than a murderer who coldly shot the father of a family. But the video doesn't lie. He was the one who fired the lethal shots.

"I didn't finish fifth grade. I left school last November, a year ago. My dad left us for another woman five years ago, and we never saw him again or knew where he went. My mom has eleven kids. Only one of them, who works in construction, sometimes brings something home for us. I used to get out of school at noon. My mom's business is making tortillas, which I would deliver to people's houses. My mom can make 300 lempiras a day, and after paying for the wood and corn, she's left with 100 a day to feed the six of us who still live with her. I'm the youngest. I left school because the tortillas had to be delivered by noon, for lunch, and if I kept on studying I couldn't deliver them on time. It was tight, we didn't want to lose clients. I only met the other kid two months ago. He's from the neighborhood. He was always standing at the corner, and started talking to me since he saw me out selling tortillas. He started saying I should go with him to steal. We were thieves. But it was only the second time I'd gone out with him to steal."

"Why did you kill the police?"

"We stole the motorcycle and were going to drop it off. The police took the keys from us. Everything happened so fast. I didn't run off because I was with him (the other kid) and because I didn't know where we were. I'd never been there, I never left my neighborhood, the Sinaí, not even to la Joya which is next door. I'd never been to the center of Tegucigalpa. I don't know anything, I didn't know where to go. There's police in front, in back, and I didn't have a license and was on a stolen motorcycle. I was trapped. That's why my friend fought back. I didn't know what to do. The gun was his, not mine. Shooting a revolver is easy, it's like magic, it shoots and that's that, it's not like a pistol, which is harder. With the tortilla work you make enough to eat rice, beans, and tortillas three times a day, but not enough to buy a cellphone, shoes, or a pair of pants. I regret it. Of course I regret it. Now they tell me I need to do eight years. When my mom comes she makes me cry. Though she hardly comes to see me because if she does she can't sell tortillas that day and makes no money and so no one can eat at home and no one has enough to pay for the transportation or to even bring me anything. I'm not a murderer, I was a thief, and I'd only been a thief for two days. Two motorcycles. I never smoked pot, or crack, or did coke in my life, not even alcohol. I was just starting. I got caught up just 'cause I was a kid."

If sentenced, Edwin will be in jail for eight years. Someone like him is lucky if he can make it that long. He was sent back to the hospital in September soon after detained. The police beat him again in the juvenile detention center of San Pedro Sula. When I saw him the first time he could hardly walk. One of the guards said that someone who kills a police officer in Honduras is "carrying four boards strapped to his back." He's the walking dead who's already sealed his fate (closing his own coffin lid) in the cycle of violence plaguing the city. Maybe that was why Edwin escaped the juvenile detention center a year later, along with 14 other members of his gang.

Joaquín, the son of the policeman, had told me, "I want to be a policeman so I can kill gangsters." But somewhere along the way, I imagine out of sadness, he turned Emo, and grew angry at me for publishing that line. He was probably right to be angry. Suyapa and Joaquín went to Tegucigalpa many times. First the government and the police paid homage to his dad during a national celebration in Honduras. Afterward, Congress gave them a certificate that deemed their father a hero. Lawmakers promised them help, housing, scholarships for the kids. But then months passed. Suyapa contacted me regularly to explain that she couldn't process her pension because she and Arita hadn't been legally married. Officially, she wasn't a widow. In reality, she didn't matter to anyone.

Four months after the murder, the day before the elections, I asked the ruling party's candidate, the president of the National Congress, Juan Orlando Hernández, about Suyapa. He made a show of ordering his campaign manager to resolve the matter immediately. He won the elections, and today he is president of Honduras. His campaign manager is now the president of the National Congress. Nothing was ever done for Suyapa.

Weeks after our meeting, Joaquín contacted me through Facebook to give me a little lecture on covering the crime beat: "If I'm being honest I hope that dog dies! I don't feel any compassion for him. And I would like to go on talking with you, but with all that's been published about me I don't trust any journalist. Good night!" Just when the shame of the journalist who reported a story, and then quickly disengaged, started to dissipate into the past, Joaquín charged at me again. "Hi Alberto. I see that in the end I was right. No one has helped me."

PART II

THE CURSE OF GEOGRAPHY

6

A LITTLE KNOWN WAR

San Pedro Sula hasn't always been where it is. Centuries ago Spanish colonialists, wanting to protect the city from constant pirate attacks, decided to move it. Today, the city is in the north of the country, about an hour from the Caribbean coast.

San Pedro Sula is organized in a grid running more horizontal than vertical; like most colonial cities, it has no skyscrapers. Outside of the city center, urbanism grows in concentric circles of poverty and marginalization, neighborhoods divorced from the downtown by highways. According to a mathematician friend of mine, these isolated barrios have levels of violence and homicide that would—if there were the slightest fall in the birthrate—completely depopulate the city in eighty-seven years.

The three-hour ride from Tegucigalpa to the Sula Valley is best done, for safety reasons, during the day. To get through the drive you have to manage traffic jams, climb over mountains, speed by an American military base, cruise through a few prairies, eat fish at Lake Yojoa, and, in the final stretch, hit a twenty-kilometer straightaway that spits you into a stunning view of the most beautiful and violent city in Honduras.

* * *

The mayor of San Pedro Sula, Juan Carlos Zúñiga, a stout and elegant young man with a finely groomed beard, used to be a surgeon. He doesn't hesitate to recognize that his city is threatened by a violence the authorities are incapable of combating. Moving the entire city again wouldn't even work; the violence in Honduras is inescapable.

My interview with the mayor is brief and formulaic. Zúñiga is tired of hearing the epithet, "most dangerous city in the world," and tries to focus on details. He does what he can, according to the manual of international cooperation, which urges him to follow certain protocols and take specified actions, but which, so far, hasn't helped. Surrounded by aides and sitting in his office on an ugly, beat-up sofa (which I read as an attempt to present a welcoming vibe) the mayor, like a broken record, churns out statistics and name-drops public projects so mechanically that once he mentions the second shelter for runaway kids, I zone out and start rereading my notes.

And my notes, I find, are full of dead bodies:

- In Honduras there are between eighty-five and ninety-one homicides per 100,000 inhabitants, depending on the local or international count. This is the favorite statistic for journalists who love to define Honduras as "the most dangerous country in the world."

- In San Pedro Sula there are 166 homicides a year per 100,000 inhabitants. This is another favorite statistic for journalists who love to define San Pedro Sula as "the most dangerous city in the world."
- The World Health Organization defines violence as epidemic if there are more than eight homicides per 100,000 inhabitants. A typical European country, like Spain, doesn't reach one homicide per 100,000 inhabitants.

Journalists are pushed to report on the most dangerous cities, the fattest officials, and the last survivor from the trenches of Normandy.

With these statistics, it makes more sense to visit the hospital than the mayor's office.

* * *

The Mario Catarino Rivas Hospital looks like a war hospital, one of those places that incites both solidarity and indignity at an international level. Honduras is suffering a forgotten and low-intensity war. The tiny old rooms in the hospital are stained with blood nobody has the time to clean up. There aren't even enough stretchers for incoming patients, and family or friends need to carry patients themselves from cars into the waiting room, or from bed to bed, or from cushion on the floor to cushion on the floor. Family members also have to wash and feed the patients themselves, buy them medicine, bandages, syringes. And to witness all this you just need to walk through the doors. With all the chaos of Honduras, needing to ask for permission is rare. The doctors have too many problems to worry about hiding anything from the press.

The doctors working in the ER that night were all student residents. Natalia Galdámez was one of them. She looked at her admittance sheet of patients who had arrived since ten that night: nineteen patients with violent injuries, most of them men between fifteen and twenty-five years old, suffering from gunshot or machete wounds. The story is always that a stranger came and, without a word of explanation, shot them—they need to fill the questionnaire box with something.

A number of the new patients that night were victims of a shootout in the Choloma pool hall. The son of one of the victims offered to take us to where, according to him, three other bodies were still sprawled on the floor. There are so many shootouts in the city that we were practically guaranteed to find bloodshed. We go. Half an hour later, we got out of the taxi we realized that the police hadn't even shown up yet, and the only people brave enough to poke their heads through the half-open door of the pool hall were a pair of teenagers with dead family members inside.

It's hard to forget the smell of blood poured out on the baize of a pool table, the size of a shotgun wound, the cups of cane liquor spilled next to the bodies, the seeming irrelevance of death, the hours that it takes to collect the bodies, the ease with which one could, if one wanted or felt it was necessary, walk in and collect all the shotgun shells. It's impossible not to be affected by the way in which evil impregnates the nights of San Pedro Sula. It's impossible not to become furious when you realize you can't get the right angle for a good photograph of the bodies. It's impossible not to be frightened in front of the bodies, the silence, the darkness, the death, the kids in the doorway and the sensation that you'd be dead if the shooters returned. It does happen. They do come back.

Despite it all, and against all logic, with the hotel an hour away and the nearest gas station a half-hour down the road, the need to piss pushed me to step into a dark corner. I whipped my head in every direction. My ears rang with terror that someone was going to appear from the shadows and catch me in a dead-end alley. I hugged the wall, took a few steps into the shadows to the only spot in which I could pee without straying too far from the others, yet not too close to the bodies that taking a piss would be disrespectful. Lifting my gaze, I spotted a little window covered over in black plastic with a hole in the middle, just big enough to see the dead bodies inside. This was the photograph we were looking for. The perfect angle.

"Esteban! Come see this!"

"God dang! That's it. Come on, move," he said, sneaking up to the window without looking at me.

"Should I make the hole wider?," I asked. "It's just plastic. I could pull the whole thing off."

"Don't even think about touching it. We can't move anything to take a photo."

Esteban Félix taught me a lot about journalism in the following two years. His photograph of the cadavers seen through the hole in black plastic earned him a World Press Photo award.

* * *

Back at the hospital, chatting with the doctor, we witnessed Natalia and her colleagues save the life of a man who'd been nearly scalped by a machete. Next, the residents removed a kidney from an old man shot in the stomach. They put the organ in a plastic bag and gave it to the man's nephew so he could take it somewhere else for analysis—an expense the hospital can't afford. Natalia, like many people in San Pedro, was fed up, exhausted. She said that with her experience she'd rather work in a war zone than stay in her own city dressing the wounds of a silent war, a war nobody wants to call a war.

* * *

Honduras is a small country cursed by geography—falling directly in the path of drugs heading to the United States; a

mule country in service of American c
a territory rented out for the pleasure of c
Sula is a rest stop and inn along the supply
to Manhattan bars and Harvard parties. A gran
Honduras costs ten dollars; in Mexico it costs t ...y dollars.
In New York, the same gram costs a hundred dollars. "If they
didn't do drugs, we wouldn't be going through what we're
going through," is the way that most locals explain it. In our
moments of nihilism, on long Honduran nights, we remember
that every line cut on the table is another death in Honduras.

San Pedro Sula shares, along with La Ceiba and the
Department of Cortés, in the border with Guatemala, a
homicide rate twice as high as the national average, and 100
times higher than the average of any European country.

According to a UN study, thirteen percent of the Honduras
GDP is tied to drug trafficking. Though in the past cocaine
made it to the US directly from Colombia, in recent years it's
been channeled through Honduras. The trend was especially
accentuated after the institutional crisis that followed the
2009 coup d'état.

In 2009, on the eve of his referendum on a constituent
assembly to change the constitution, President Manuel Zelaya
was pushed out of bed by the barrel of a gun. His attempt at
constitutional change was considered by many to be inspired by
Venezuela's late Hugo Chavez. That was when those in charge of
maintaining the law plunged into complete chaos. They focused

.r efforts on establishing a new government and repressing the opposition instead of stopping the "narco-flights." The United States and the European Union subsequently suspended their drug trafficking assistance programs. Not a single country in the world recognized the coup government. One of the immediate consequences of the coup was a sort of cocaine gold rush. Planes loaded with the drug took direct flights through Honduras. Since the coup, ninety percent of cocaine entering the United States passes through Central America.

Emilio Ulloa manages security for Dole, the largest banana company in the world and largest landowner in the Caribbean. With the open sincerity of a witness who feels his hands are tied, he explains how the company's fumigation plane runways were used as narco-runways at least four times before the coup, between 2006 and 2008. Groups of up to forty heavily armed men came in trucks, overpowered and restrained the single guard, who typically carried nothing but a revolver, and unloaded the merchandise from the plane. "The fight was never fair," he complained. "The narcos attack and there isn't even resistance." It's asymmetrical warfare. On one side, the poorly outfitted and miserably paid Honduran police; on the other side, well-armed killers guarding multi-million dollar shipments.

More than just another strand of disorder, drug trafficking is the dynamo that sparks all the violence the country suffers. It works like a multinational company generating employment through local subcontracting; a multinational so powerful that it ends up penetrating and corrupting all existing state structures.

Thanks to cocaine, the border between common delinquency and organized crime has evaporated in recent years. Assassinations, trafficking crimes, and the "settling of accounts" are now carried out by the gangs that used to steal cellphones and rob banks. This shift is taking place, in part, because cartels are paying for smuggling in drugs instead of in dollars. It's both easier and cheaper for them. In order to maintain control over their workers, owners have long paid them in products or discounts. The result is a low-intensity war between gangs—bands of small-time dealers, extortionists, and security forces that cross back and forth over the thin line between law and criminality.

In Honduras we have yet to see a war for control of the trafficking routes, as we've seen in Mexico between competing cartels. Isolated incidents aside, there aren't massacres of twelve or more people, or systematic decapitations, or bodies dissolved in acid, as we've seen in Mexico. But what we do see in Honduras, just as we see in Mexico, is innocent victims caught in the crossfire between the army, the narcos, gangs and the police.

7

MOSQUITO COAST

1. THE PLACE

Gracias a Dios (Thank God), the official name of the Mosquito Coast, is a department of Honduras so remote that not even adventure tourists find it. Most of Gracias a Dios is covered in a mixture of mangrove jungle, swamps, and flood plains. There's only one dirt highway, impossible to navigate for part of the year, connecting the region's capital, Puerto Lempira, with a few remote farms. The rest of the area is only accessible by plane, helicopter, or motorized canoes, known locally as *pipantes*, which navigate through rivers turned into fluvial highways.

The dense La Mosquitia jungle is also a paradise of small runways for planes taking off from Venezuela and Colombia loaded with cocaine. The runways can be cleared and constructed in less than twenty-four hours with the help of men in nearby villages, who earn in a day clearing runways what they would usually earn in a month.

At dawn on the morning of 11 May 2012, four bodies were discovered near the Paptalaya pier.

For photographer Rodrigo Abd and me, the Mosquito Coast was hard to get to. Though at first unsure if the reports of human rights abuses we were hearing were credible, if they were propaganda or factual, we were finally convinced these events had indeed taken place, though they'd only been reported on by a few activist bloggers. The fact that the *New York Times* was en route didn't hurt, as battles for a first scoop still invigorate this field a little bit. The easy part was buying plane tickets from Tegucigalpa to La Ceiba and renting a plane the size of a Fiat Panda to cruise over that mix of humid forest and swamp dotted with runways. Also a cinch was dealing with Rodrigo, who had to ask the pilot to lean his seat back so he could snap photos—a necessary sacrifice in seeking an edge over his competitors by catching the unique image. Asking about what actually happened was where the difficulties set in.

II. THE FACTS

Before dawn on 11 May 2012, Celin Eriksson, seventeen years old, waited on the Paptalaya pier for his family members, due in shortly on a *pipante*. His family had told Celin that there would be work that night, unloading a plane on a nearby runway, but he'd decided to pass over the hundred dollars he would have made. Some other neighbors, however, did take the job. It's easy work: unloading drugs from the plane onto a vehicle, getting paid, and then disappearing. The rest is taken care of by the narcos, who are typically Mexican. They're the ones who then drive the merchandise into town and load it onto a *pipante* at the same pier where Celin was waiting for his family. That early May morning, when Celin saw a group of forty narcos arriving in a caravan, he decided that the best thing to do was to hide. It wasn't out of fear—he was used to living with narcos—but simple prudence.

At the same time Celin was waiting for his family, American Drug Enforcement Agency officers, along with Honduran police, were searching the Paptalaya area by helicopter. The agents observed a group of men carrying bundles of drugs on the pier and they decided to intervene: a few masked commandos descending by rope from the helicopter and securing the area without firing their weapons. Before fleeing, however, the narcos had pushed the boat off the pier, hoping to recover it later.

The helicopter landed in front of Sandra Madrid's house, the biggest building near the Paptalaya pier, which functioned as a sundry shop and ticket office for passengers looking for *pipante* rides up or down the river. Six agents kicked through the door, pushed Sandra's husband to the floor, and kept a gun against his head for two hours as they demanded to know if he was "El Renco," or if he worked for "El Renco," or if the drugs were "El Renco's." Two Honduran police officers and one DEA agent boarded a *pipante*, finding a motor and gas in Madrid's house, and took off down the river. The rest of the agents went on to interrogate the neighbors.

Celin had witnessed the masked men dangling down from the helicopters. He was scared that if they saw him hiding they would mistake him for a narco and shoot, so the best thing, he figured, was to make himself conspicuous. The soldiers detained him and repeated the scene they'd rehearsed in Madrid's house: they pointed a gun at his head, threatened to kill him, and asked him about "El Renco." After his interrogation, the masked men forced him to walk along the shore of the river to look for the drug boat, in case it had run aground. After walking about a kilometer, the agents received a radio order to stop their search. They left Celin handcuffed in the dark and told him not to move.

As Celin was sitting with his hands cuffed along the bank of the river, another *pipante* approached the pier. It was full of stacks of plastic chairs, vegetables to be sold in the market, and locals dozing in their seats. Among the passengers were Tom Brooks and his mother, Clara Woods, who Celin had been planning to welcome at the pier and accompany to their house. At the same time, the police officers who'd stormed Sandra Madrid's house were nervously motoring around, barely able to steer their *pipante*, and looking in vain through the darkness for the boat that the narcos had pushed adrift.

Then, suddenly, in front of them, appeared a boat full of packages. They were scared. They knew that the narcos were close and were willing to defend their cargo. They radioed to the helicopter to ask for aerial backup. And then the shooting began. First from the helicopter. Then from the police in the *pipante*, emptying their cartridges in the direction of the plastic chairs, the market vegetables, and the dozing passengers. Four of them were killed.

Sitting handcuffed along the bank of the river, Celin could hear the gunshots.

III. THE DEAD

Hilda Lezama, the owner of the boat that came under attack (twelve meters long, with seating for twenty-five), recalls the event in a hospital bed in the Morava mission in Ahuas, a nearby town. In her right leg she has a bullet hole big enough to put a fist through. "War wounds like I saw in Iraq," the American missionary doctor working at the hospital said to me. Lezama had been dozing, like most of the other passengers. Then the sound of a helicopter woke her seconds before the shooting began. She says that the first burst of gunfire came from the air, and then the helicopter took two turns before firing two more bursts. When survivors started swimming for the shore, the helicopter shot a flare to be able to see and find them again. Why didn't they shoot the flare before firing? Lucio Nelson, who suffered various wounds to the back and arms, and Wilmer Lucas, who lost a hand in the attack, told me the same story from their hospital beds in La Ceiba. Darkness, noise, gunfire from the air, and then: light and water. Hilda, Lucio, and Wilmer had more luck than Tom Brooks, Celin's cousin. Tom was killed, along with Emerson Martínez, Candelaria Trapp, and Juana Jackson. None of the survivors recall having seen the boat with the agents. The thundering of the helicopter rotors prevented them from even hearing the gunshots. All of them confirm that nobody in the boat shot towards the helicopter, or was even armed.

A few days later I went to see the *pipante* moored to the landing for repairs. I counted twenty bullet holes in the bottom and side walls of the boat. A few of the holes were big enough to fit two or three of my fingers through. Despite the fact that witnesses claimed the shots came from helicopters, according to the autopsies of the four murdered victims, the shots came from a level height, with entry and exit wounds along horizontal lines. According to the Public Prosecutor's Office, it was the American and two Honduran agents who were inside a boat who killed the victims while looking for the drug boat. The crucial question is: was it the Honduran agents or the American agent who fired the shots? American agents are not authorized to fire their weapons, except in a case of legitimate defense. And it seems there was no reason for self-defense in this case.

IV. THE CONTEXT

When the Army finds a narco-runway, it sends in the entire team from Tegucigalpa. Soldiers descend from helicopters, set the dynamite, and blow it all up. In response, the narcos return to fill in the holes, or, if the damage is more extensive, build another lane next to the old one. It's quick and easy: with a simple tractor you can build a runway in less than twenty-four hours.

In this back-and-forth war, the narcos always win. They have geography on their side, as well as the general poverty of the region. Plus, the police and Army lack basic resources.

The mayor of Ahuas, Lucio Baquedano, has tried repeatedly to convince villagers not to help build runways close to their land. "But nobody listens to us," he says, frustrated. "I can't go against the people. They don't have other job opportunities."

The man who housed and fed us during our stay in Ahuas, Gerald Rivera, said that the people of this area were poor and spent their days sitting around. He himself was poor, and spent his days sitting around. He explained that the little fieldwork available was only enough to keep from going hungry. The only other available job was diving for lobsters—dangerous work that many young people refused to do. There are fewer lobsters these days, and the scarcity requires divers to swim ever deeper. Plus, the lack of proper equipment and the hurry to resurface and pull in more lobsters per day has resulted in more incidents of decompression sickness. Divers are increasingly dying or becoming paralyzed. Understandably, many of them harbor resentment: "With half the price they pay for one of those helicopters, they could build a factory where we could work, and the problems in the villages would be solved."

The relation between poverty and falling in with the narcos is so obvious that even high-ranking police officers speak the language of community activism. This is exactly how Police Commissioner Bonilla talks about it. He can point to the problem as easily as the president can, or the colonel, or any village teenager can point to the problem. "There isn't work, or sanitation, or education. These villagers have been abandoned by the state, which doesn't have the resources to invest in them. With no state, someone else showed up and invested, offering a minimum wage for runway construction and unloading jobs. The narcos drop into these isolated villages and bring supplies, medicine, electric generators, and solar panels. If the state fulfilled this role, the Miskitos wouldn't let the narcos in—they know it's illegal and that sooner or later problems will arise. Plus, though the narcos may seem giving at first, later they resort to pressuring and threatening the villagers. The problem isn't that they're building runways. The problem is the narcos themselves, who are not in Moskitia, but in Tegucigalpa and San Pedro Sula, in Bogata, Caracas, and Miami. You better believe it."

Filiberto Pravia couldn't stop laughing. He approaches life calmly and with a sense of humor, though the first impression he gives—pulling his shotgun out from underneath his black full-length trench coat—might make you a little nervous. He's perfected the motion of revealing his shotgun in front of the mirror, studying Clint Eastwood's movements in some of his old low-budget Westerns. Pravia is as unassuming (despite the gun) as he is caring and welcoming to guests. He was staying in the same hotel as the journalists, though who knows what kind of deal he had with the owner, who wasn't charging him. He's the chief of the three police officers who are headquartered in an adobe shack and charged to maintain law and order, armed with nothing but three pistols, one sawn-off shotgun, and thirty bullets. For transportation, they have to rely on rides from the mayor's office. Pravia explained that nobody could really expect them to confront the groups of up to fifty heavily armed men that often guard a drug shipment. He doesn't want to get involved in massacres, and when someone lets him know that narcos are passing through, the police simply shut themselves in and wait for the problem to go away. Commissioner Bonilla offers a depressing statistic: in a territory of 16,000 square kilometers with a population of 88,000, there are only sixty police officers, forty of whom are stationed in the state headquarters, in Puerto Lempira, with the other twenty spread out over all of Moskitia, equipped with neither boats nor cars.

On the night in question, Filiberto heard the helicopters and went to the river to see what was going on. When he arrived, at dawn, he saw some of the villagers setting fire to the houses of people they claimed had organized the drug shipment. "What am I going to do to stop angry villagers armed with machetes and gasoline? I was lucky to escape." Pravia offered the same Intel that Honduran Army and US DEA agents had—that the narco's name was Renco.

"Since the whole thing led back to 'El Renco,'" Pravia said, "family and friends of the people who were murdered went to torch the houses of the narcos who started the whole problem." But nobody had information about who, exactly, El Renco was. In Honduras, people keep their mouths shut when it comes to narcos. Somebody burned four houses. Who? The villagers. Why? "Because we're fed up." The only other answer they give is silence, or the conclusive: "They'll finish me if I speak to you." The burned houses will never be rebuilt. The village had asked them not to run shipments so close. But they didn't listen. And problems arose. Popular justice was the only option. Journalism in narco zones is simple. It's typically sufficient to cast a quick glance or to conduct an interview, being sure not to ask for too many names. Did the authorities know all this before four innocent civilians were murdered? Of course they did. The whole world knew it. Could they have avoided these deaths if they had a functioning state? Probably, yes.

V. THE CONSEQUENCES

The US government opened an internal investigation, but declined to release the helicopter video of the operation. Investigators never informed Honduran officials of the conclusions from the DEA report, or told them what weapons the US agents in the *pipante* were carrying. The only information journalists received from Washington was the repeated claim of self-defense, which superseded any question of motive: the agents were defending themselves against an aggression, and the DEA did not participate in the shootout. The guilt, of course, lay elsewhere. It was a classic defense.

There was chatter for a few months. An investigation led by the Honduran Prosecutor's Office, delegations of American human rights NGOs, press conferences, and articles in American newspapers scrutinizing every detail of that night. And, as always, there was a lot of gossip. The Human Rights groups claimed from the first day that two of the murdered women were pregnant. This added an extra element to the tragedy (not only civilians, but pregnant civilians) though it jeopardized their credibility as they weren't able to prove that the women were pregnant. They persisted in their claims to the extent that, months later, two prosecutors and a forensic scientist took a US-funded helicopter flight to disinter the cadavers—which were already partially decomposed in the humid soil—to certify that there were no fetuses. That lie, or perhaps that truth that was impossible to verify, was enough for some to doubt the veracity of the entire story. I'll never know if they were exaggerating or not, if they were lying or if it was true that the women were pregnant, but I have no doubt that the activists' lack of precision, as well-intentioned as they may have been, did nothing to help. And still, the journalist who feels a duty to report only proven fact and to resist speculation becomes, in the eyes of human rights defenders, an agent of empire.

Honduran prosecutors didn't come through. Even though they wanted to (or they probably wanted to), they weren't able to do a thing. Prosecutors asked their American counterparts for the interviews they conducted with the US agents involved in the operation. They never received them. They asked for a list of the weapons used in the shooting so that they could do a ballistic analysis and determine who fired the lethal shots. They never received the list. The prosecutors finally threw in the towel. They weren't going to confront the governments of both Honduras and the US when officials from neither country were willing to work with them.

More than delivering justice to the victims, Hondurans were worried about losing the economic and military support of their northern neighbor. The Leahy Law, named after Democratic Vermont Senator Patrick Leahy, requires the US State Department to cancel aid packages destined for foreign military or police units if they've been shown to commit human rights violations. That's to say, if US money is being used to kill Honduran civilians boating along a river, the aid should be suspended. This leads to the poor receiving country losing access to helicopters, military advisors, radar systems, and jet fuel.

After the incident in Ahuas, Senator Leahy's office asked for details about what had happened, and the Senator was not pleased with the responses. In order to continue with the military aid package it called for a public investigation and made a series of demands, which were never met. The principal demand—the first on the list—as well as the only one that didn't have to do with an investigation, was to compensate the victims and recognize that they had been killed in error, a demand also made by the Honduran police commission, which had written a report about the incident. And yet: "Honduran authorities don't want to offer an example or set a precedent," Tim Rieser, Senator Leahy's top aide, told me in Washington. Rieser and Leahy decided that Operation Anvil, which put the US advisors on helicopters, would not continue, and that was that. A few DEA agents lost their posts. No helicopter financed by the United States, at least not publicly financed, has participated in drug interdiction operations in La Mosquitia since.

After the massacre in Ahuas and the suspension of Operation Anvil, Honduras dusted off an old "pragmatic" idea that the Army and the political class had long been interested in: shoot down the narco planes. It is illegal according to international law, so as a consequence of the strategic shift, the US also canceled its radar technology program, which it had been sharing with Honduran intelligence. The results were disastrous: in 2011 Honduran Army and police forces decommissioned about twenty tons of cocaine; the number dropped to six tons in 2012, and only two tons in 2013.

The Honduran government not only refused to back down from its strategy of shooting down planes, they actually turned it into a law. In 2014 Parliament legally sanctioned the shooting down of unapproved non-military aircraft flying in La Mosquitia by night. "Honduras maintains the right to defend its sovereignty, and it is Honduran law that should apply, not US law," the president and his security ministers explained to me one morning. Assuming that the moment they actually do shoot down a plane the US would refuse, once again, to share radar information with Honduras, the government decided to spend $25 million to purchase new radar equipment from Israel.

Gabriel García Márquez, in his Nobel Prize acceptance speech, "The Solitude of Latin America," said: "The immeasurable violence and pain in our history are the result of long-simmering injustices and untold bitterness, not a conspiracy plotted 3,000 leagues from our home."

PART III

HOUSES, COFFINS, AND GRAFFITI

8

REFUGEE CAMP

Alejandro Durón is not a taxi driver, he isn't a jungle-dwelling indigenous man, or a *maquila* assembly-line worker in the conflict-ridden suburbs of San Pedro Sula. He's a thirty-four-year-old systems analyst with whom I often go to happy hour after an outing at Tegucigalpa's Spanish Cultural Center. Over drinks one afternoon, Alejandro told me how he'd recently come home to find an envelope stuck under his door. It demanded a payment of 50,000 lempiras (about $2,500). In the note, the extortionists described Alejandro's routines. They'd been watching him. "If you don't pay, they can kill you," Alejandro said without hesitation. If you pay once, they'll never leave you in peace.

The day he found the envelope, Alejandro and his partner, Helen, decided they wouldn't go home. They slept elsewhere and asked a neighbor to feed their dog. They didn't return to their home for a week, and then only for a few hours, to pick up their things. Then they left behind their house—the invested savings, the mortgage, the plans, the room for the baby they didn't yet have, the room where they kept their movie and book collections, their work and the memories of a lifetime together—for the rental home they've lived in ever since. Of course, they never reported the incident. "Why should we?," Helen asked herself. "To risk bumping into our extortionist at the police station?"

Alejandro and Helen's situation is not exceptional. When I started to ask around, I discovered that many people knew someone who had gone through something similar.

Cecilia, who works for an international organization in Tegucigalpa, told me that in the space of less than a month she'd received a phone call at work and two more calls at her house demanding money. They knew the ins and outs of her morning and evening routines. She changed her phone numbers and tried to forget about the problem. Nothing happened to her. But for many months she walked around the city full of anxiety. A Spanish neighbor decided to go back to his home after getting one such call. A pharmacist friend asked an NGO for help in dealing with an extortionist gang member. She had to pay her extortion in favors: she'd been a police officer in the past and still had a lot of connections with the police—connections that helped her get an inmate gang member released. Some pay in blood. Others flee.

We're all potential victims in a country where victim-ization is the rule instead of the exception. Telephonic extortion in the capital with the highest homicide rate in the world is something almost no one can escape; the folded piece of paper under the door is all the more terrifying because it implies physical proximity. Sometimes it's a jailed gang member that commits these extortions. One only needs to look through the phone book and call at random. The method of trial and error works—a matter of probability. There's always someone who will get scared and pay. The extortionists can also be neighbors, co-workers, offended friends, all of them with valuable information about the victim. Those who've recently inherited or sold property, those with a family member abroad who sends remittances, those who work for an international organization and get paid in dollars—all are potential prey to a gangster trying to score an easy buck. To the list of possible extortionists we should add the police. If an inmate can extort from jail, what couldn't a police officer do—an armed officer with access to valuable information?

Helen and Alejandro are political activists, hardened by their resistance to the coup d'état, and, as such, they're used to threats and tension. Unlike the great majority of Hondurans who remain silent, they decided to tell their story on the record. They speak in order to resist. Every year there are fewer people who remember the Tegucigalpa from before the Reign of Hell. Remembering "the good times" is important to them. Alejandro remembers how eight years ago, when he needed to make a decision about something important, he'd go out for a walk or get on a bus and meander through the city for an entire afternoon. Now he doesn't walk. It's been eight years since he's walked about the city or has intermingled beyond what he calls his "circle of confidence." In Honduras the concept of community no longer exists, not beyond certain circles that are very private, familial, or work-centered, in which everyone knows each other. This dynamic exacerbates a societal alienation and fragmentation where social groups are increasingly shrinking, paranoid, and irremediably disconnected from one another. In Honduras your words, attitudes and answers are weighed against the fear that someone else may see or hear you. Because of a reckless celebration at a café, a loud toast over someone's promotion, or a secret told to a co-worker, life can unfold into a nightmare.

The problems in Honduras are micro and macro, come from the left and the right, attack from afar and nearby, affect the poor and the middle class. In a well-oiled state one is taught to see taxes as a foul-tasting medicine: they make one gag, but they cure the illness. Every month we put money into the communal pot so that, sooner or later, we can pull from it when we need to go to the hospital or college. In Honduras, however, the great collector is not the state, but the extortionist. Violence is born out of the intense competition for that pot of money.

As usual, following a professional protocol created many years ago and many kilometers away from Tegucigalpa, I went to talk with the police. As if a corrupt and dysfunctional police officer could ever be a credible source.

* * *

To get to the public relations office of the police headquarters of Tegucigalpa you need to enter through a door that looks like it will lead you into a corner store. Through the door are willing, smiling, and approachable officers who serve clients with the hospitality that is so abundant in administrative offices in Honduras, and which is so hard to penetrate without compromising your dignity. Public relations liaison Ana Velasquez sat in the building's lobby amidst an arrangement of family portraits, plastic flowers, and porcelain kittens—all of them perfectly arranged around her. It's nothing more than a passé, 1970s-style foyer for the department of propaganda. Honduras hasn't yet upgraded its communication gurus and PR specialists to model 2.0.

In offices such as these a foreign journalist is like exotic game. A few phrases— "I'm a reporter for …," or "I'm from …."—are enough for all the doors to open and all the office priorities to realign. For them, the bourgeois foreign journalist is the ideal spokesperson to whitewash their image. They're anxious to break the isolating seal of antipathy separating them from the society they promise to protect.

"What can I help you with?"

"Well, you see, I'm working on an article about people who have to leave their homes because of gang extortion and I'd like to…"

"You couldn't have come at a better time."

I'm not even able to finish my sentence. My accent and the mere mention of a foreign publisher have propelled the PR liaison to call her boss, Chief of Police Harold Bonilla, and arrange an interview immediately.

"The chief is waiting for you, follow me."

"But I don't want to inconvenience anyone, I just want to…"

Before realizing it, I enter a modest and practical office, the office of a man of order—a military officer. A room with four men sitting, drinking iced tea, and passing the time until they're interrupted by an unexpected guest. They solicitously stand to welcome me. I feel uneasy. This, I realize, will not be an interview.

The first thing to come out of the huge mouth of the tiny chief of police is a blue dental retainer that eliminates any remaining aura of gravity. Tegucigalpa's chief of police, aside from fighting gangs and organized crime, is correcting his bite. I don't dare ask him if it's for aesthetics. At his side is the ever simpatico Detective Barahona, head of the community and neighborhood policing program, one of those subordinates who endlessly parrots the words of his boss. Barahona is a morbidly obese man who struggles to get up off the sofa and to whom, of course, I don't dare say it's unnecessary to do so.

Over the next hour Bonilla will repeatedly refer to the other two men in the room as "representatives of the private sector." And just as many times, he will reiterate that the police, lacking funds, cannot lower the city's rate of violence without their economic contributions. They work for Lafisse Bank and the private security company SGS. I decide not to ask them their names or exchange cards so as not to discomfit them more than I already have with my impromptu visit.

Just like his PR liaison, Police Chief Bonilla doesn't let me explain what I'm looking for. You might call me a captive journalist—temporarily held captive from reality. But, I tell myself, I should be able to glean something useful from the meeting. I know they're not interested in answering my questions about people abandoning their houses because of gang extortion.

The chief of police morphs into a true politician, answering all my questions with thorough euphemism: "Violence shouldn't only be studied through its manifestations, but also in a holistic manner, and this is why we're trying to change the culture of the country. This is what we want to show you." I begin to see their true colors: they're going to use PowerPoint as a shield and refuse to answer any questions. Doubtless pleased with my captivity, Bonilla goes overboard, unlike his visitors, and calls for more drinks, as well as a projector. What was going to be an informal chat with a public official and his financiers has turned into—after a hard-fought battle untangling the computer cables—a long and boring slideshow presentation. There's no way to escape. I remain trapped until the end of the spectacle.

For Bonilla, the solution to violence is, as he calls it, "holistic focus": getting leaders of various neighborhoods to meet with the police in order to break the ice and convince them of the great gains of collaboration and community work. Meetings that, of course, cost money, money that the police force doesn't have and that the private sector should provide so that security can thrive in Tegucigalpa.

Detective Barahona, far from an expert in the fight against gangs—the police force's most obscure (and failing) battle on the face of this continent—explains that recovering houses occupied by gang members "is just part of the operation, the easiest part, accomplished by sending a large group of agents to those areas." They're called operations of saturation. The police arrive in full force at the scene, wailing their sirens. But they arrive too late, allowing the "*Banderas*," the kids who keep a lookout, to flee in every direction and warn their big brothers: "The cops are here. The cops are here." The agents stay out of trouble by affording the gang members a few minutes to flee. They never catch anybody; at most they'll seize a token AK-47 to show the press. They bother the neighborhood for a couple of hours, putting all the youngsters against a wall and slapping them around in vain, breaking down a couple of wooden doors, turning over a couple of houses. They'll call the press over once the scene has been prepped, and then they're off.

In any case, the real work, the work that actually brings peace to a neighborhood, happens through collaboration with neighbors, or, in PowerPoint lingo, by making alliances with the community. Bonilla and Barahona say they're responsible for the fact that, in 2011, the Barrio 18 gang abandoned 400 occupied houses in the neighborhood of Planeta in San Pedro Sula.

As proof, they show photos, "from a USB we seized from a gangster." In the photos you can see gang members posing in front of huge murals full of letters and snakes, armed with AK-47s, Galils, and mini Uzis, photos of abandoned houses, shuttered businesses, and of what they call the slaughter-house: a room full of blood, strewn clothes—where they executed their victims. To underscore this important police success, they show me photos of Barahona posing in the same locations, now liberated, with the ease and relaxed good-naturedness with which he'd pose in front of the Tower of Pisa or the Egyptian pyramids.

The officers point out the graffiti. The gang had swapped the gothic 18s they would tag everywhere to claim their territory for huge peaceful landscape murals and biblical messages. "It turns out the only murals they won't destroy are those inspired by the Lord," they explain. "This always works. They'll fight the police but don't dare fight God." Bonilla attributes everything to the hand of God. A flag of Israel hangs over his office and another waves in the background of his Blackberry screen. He's part of one of those evangelical sects that have overtaken the area and respond to every situation by urging victims to kneel with their arms reaching up to the heavens, palms up, their faces in a trance as they sing terrible songs. Maybe that's why they always have that dreamy smile on their faces.

But the mural that glorifies God and paints the police as His intermediary on Earth, of course, costs money. The food and refreshments offered at the community meeting they've called for the following Sunday in the Buenos Aires neighborhood, of course, cost money. Money the police don't have. That's why the private sector, which has applauded the presentation, has come to collaborate with the police.

As people begin to fidget with their iPhones, and WhatsApp messages begin to flash, the presentation spikes to a climax. Ana Velasquez procures a camera from her purse. The chief of police stretches his flag of Israel over the table so that it's visible, and everyone willingly gets up to pose for a picture. But, of course, not without first catching me in their trap.

"Mr. Journalist, your presence here is a great opportunity for you to attest to this very important moment. Come closer and give witness," the chief of police tells me.

"You know I really shouldn't, Chief. This is well beyond my job description."

"Don't worry, you're among men of faith. Everything here is by the book and we work under the name of God. And anyway, you're already a part of this divine project. You're now one of us."

Embarrassed, lowering my face and covering it with my notebook as much as possible, I pretend I'm writing, though in reality I'm hiding so that no one will identify me in the paper tomorrow. The worst thing is not that the private sector has given a token of support—a bundle of 500-lempira bills, without any receipt or documentation—to the chief of police of Tegucigalpa. Nor that the chief claims, as he sticks the wad of bills in his pocket, that the Church will oversee the proper use of this donation. The worst thing by far is that this picture could wind up all over the Honduran press tomorrow, making me a participant in this shady business.

Once the private sector has left, I feign ignorance and simply go on with my work. I want to know if they can get me access to a neighborhood where gangs are occupying houses. I try to convince them to let me go to their Sunday meeting; that I'd like to enjoy the sodas and empanadas they'll no doubt purchase with those fifteen 500-lempira notes now wedged into the pocket of the chief of police of Tegucigalpa.

"On Sunday, in the neighborhood of Buenos Aires, we'll put out an urn in which neighbors can leave anonymous notes telling us what they never dare officially report. And I'll find you someone willing to talk; there's always someone, don't worry. You can count on me."

Bonilla and Barahona proceed to "Thank God for the miracle of their new ally." Bonilla grabs me by the hand, Barahona grabs my other hand, and together we form a celestial triangle. Bonilla improvises a prayer thanking God for a journalist willing to collaborate with him on this project. Every two or three phrases, Barahona lets go of his boss' hand and elevates it to the sky like a reveler at a gospel concert, whispering, "Help us, Lord."

It seems the doors to the police mentality have been opened for me, the only thing is that I'm not sure anyone has turned the lights on.

Days later, the community meeting—financed in cash by the private sector under the nose of a journalist—has still not taken place. The meeting was to be held at nine on a Sunday morning at the police station of a neighborhood Tegucigalpa. After waiting around a few hours that Sunday, I gave up. The district agents had never heard of any meeting; nor had the neighbors. No one showed.

The next Monday I had time to go back to the city's chief of police to demand an explanation for standing me up. The PR liaison, Ana Velásquez, defended the office with a classically irrefutable argument: "Scheduling problems." And she got rid of me, directing me to the office of Deputy Chief of Police Miguel Martinez Madrid. "He can help you, he has a

TV show. I don't know if you've seen 'Cops' on TV. He really understands the needs of the press."

The public relations agent had a point. Martinez Madrid is the perfect example of someone a journalist would consider a good source. Young, elegant, educated, conceited, he's like a clean-cut cop from the 1950s, but his office looks like that of a high-class lawyer or doctor, not that of a policeman. His societal diagnosis seems more focused than that of his superiors. His comportment is typical of second-tier public employees, those who participate in the system without changing one comma in its narrative. I don't think they're any more honest than their bosses, though they might be less hypocritical. At least they don't dodge questions or try to hide the truth.

In Martinez Madrid's reality, despite the grave displacements of people, no one—not the police, nor the Public Ministry, nor the United Nations Office in Honduras—is capable of giving exact numbers. The number of houses occupied by the gangs is on the rise in Tegucigalpa, but that's not the case for the number of reported incidents. "Though we have Intelligence information on the areas where a problem has been detected, we can't clear out houses if we don't have complaints," Martinez Madrid admits.

The victims have become invisible refugees without any campaigns to support them, surviving without the solidarity of European NGOs. Not even the victims themselves see themselves as refugees. For that to happen, someone would have to acknowledge that the country is at war.

The same night I spoke with Martinez Madrid, eighty-two-year-old Oscon Armando Ochoa didn't get the chance to run from his extortionists. They shot him seven times, point blank, inside his own home.

* * *

Francisco Moncada lives in the center of Tegucigalpa, a few blocks from the Parque Central. Every night he gets together with some neighbors to talk and smoke cigarettes or to take their dogs out for a walk. For many years he hasn't been able to do this without carrying a gun. He has one of the prettiest houses in the neighborhood, built in the 1940s, and he says he won't dare paint it for fear that gangs would notice his socioeconomic status and start extorting him, which is exactly what happened to a neighboring business. The gang demanded 20,000 lempiras (about $1,000), and the business paid it. "This was once a pretty area, where one could sit or stroll, now it's full of ruins and trash. Tegucigalpa is a dead city."

Moncada got so scared when he saw my published article that he decided to write me this message: "I remember having that conversation in our neighborhood, in front of my house, but, to be frank, you never asked me for an interview, nor did you ask for my permission to publish what we talked about. I think exposing my case just to get a few more lines for your story was dangerous and reckless, I gave you the trust fit for a foreigner, I opened the doors to my house, I never gave you an interview. If I shared my worries about painting or not painting my house, it was only so that you see our reality, not for you to expose me. If you were at risk, you'd book a flight out of here. If I start getting extorted, I would have to save for an entire year to get out of here. Think about what you did."

As a journalist, my conscious is clear. I followed the rules in identifying myself, explaining that I was looking for impressions about door-to-door extortions, and I spent a good amount of time with him taking notes, notebook in hand, asking him for details of his situation and biography. But as a person, of course, my conscience is not clear. If something were to happen to him, I'd blame myself. His fear is mine.

9

ONE COFFIN, ONE VOTE

I was looking for information about a murder, but instead I found coffins.

I'd gone to the Tegucigalpa municipal morgue, one of those daily journalistic pilgrimages one makes to compile reactions, check quotes, or look for sources to explain what's happening. It's the central hub for the two biggest commodities of Honduras: poverty and death.

At the morgue, I found myself with Luis Membreño, crying uncontrollably for his nineteen-year-old brother Marvin, who was murdered with three shots to the head a few hours previously in a neighborhood on the outskirts of the city. Next to him were relatives of Marco Almendárez, a fifty-two-year-old security guard, and the family of José Jamaca, twenty-nine years old; both were murder victims.

In that sad group of people one person stood out. Her name is Carla Majano and, though she appeared to be visibly grieving, she was not a relative, or a neighbor of one of the families, but a politician. Working for the city's Office of the Environment, she goes to the morgue to act as a "liaison" for the poorest families, helping those who would otherwise be forced to bury their loved ones in a sheet to obtain access to free coffins and candles. Carrying a stack of folders and two cellphones, she explained that in less than half a year she's put forty-five families in contact with the "Mortuary of the People."

In other countries, politicians trying to win the votes of the most humble populations will give away new shoes or aluminum sheets to build roofs for shacks; in Honduras they give away coffins and fund funerals. Honduras—a funeral home with its own flag and constitution.

The program didn't grow out of the crime wave washing over Honduras, but as part of the political campaign of Ricardo Alvarez, the mayor of Tegucigalpa. The Mortuary of the People works out of a rundown office, dusty and invaded by the streetside traffic roar, a few steps from the capital's historic center. It's full of coffins of every type and size (grey for adults, white for kids), boxes of candles, and packaged snacks. The budget is 150,000 lempiras a month (some $7,600). The coffin for the Membreño family is the 701st coffin that the funeral home has given away this year; since it was established, in 2006, the funeral home has given away almost 5,000 coffins.

Free coffins mean loss of profits for private funeral homes: the cheapest coffin runs at 2,500 lempiras ($125), to which you have to add the cost of transportation, the cost of the burial plot, and the cost of installation. The package deal of a private funeral home, with the funeral service included, can climb upwards of 20,000 lempiras (around $1,000), and the minimum salary in Honduras is fixed at 6,000 lempiras a month ($300). The Mortuary of the People offers the same, but for zero lempiras.

Jose Gutierrez, employee of the Funeral Home of Santa Rita, next door to the municipal morgue, complains that politicians have given his business unfair competition. "We're salesmen, of course, but we have a heart; when a very poor family can't pay, we call the free funeral service ourselves."

But this commercial battle isn't only between the Mortuary of the People and the private funeral services. The political program is so successful that when an electoral campaign is near, imitators pop up. The funereal politics of businessman and aspiring mayor Tito Asfura are less demanding, and more arbitrary, than those of the current mayor. Asfura successfully circumvented the municipal bureaucracy that weighs down the inner workings of the Mortuary of the People.

"Tito Asfura does it better than Ricardo Alvarez. He doesn't ask any questions or demand paperwork. He even chips in for gas and, sometimes, food," explains Felipe Leon, another "friend" who waits at the door of the morgue to receive the body of Jamaca and take it to the cemetery.

The third competitor is the president of the National Congress, Juan Orlando Hernandez (currently the president of Honduras). His program "Coming Back Home" has national reach and covers the cost of transportation from the place of death to the morgue, whether that's a block away or to the jungle of Mosquitia. This is the model the family of the third victim, Marco Almendarez, chooses. Almendarez was from the city of Comayagua, and didn't qualify for either of the first two funeral services.

The money comes out of a congressional expense fund (or "reptile fund"), which doesn't have to be disclosed. Some politicians give away coffins, others pay for the European Master's degrees of their friends' kids or the Miami shopping sprees of their neighborhood political operatives.

And, of course, one can always stoop lower.

* * *

At dawn, in front of the morgue, there are three pickups full of bodies wrapped in white plastic bags. The deliverymen want to finish quickly, and aren't doing much talking. When the caravan gets to the city cemetery, only two journalists are there to observe the officers stacking the bodies on the floor. The teeth of a mechanical shovel tear some of the bags open: an arm falls out, a limb peeks through, and the green liquid of the decomposing bodies spills over the lid of the pit. A priest says a blessing and sprinkles holy water over the bodies. Almost no one wants to watch. No families are present. "It might be that there was a miscommunication, that they haven't been informed of the death, or that they simply don't have the money to pay for the cost and they're embarrassed to show up now. It can also be that they just don't know, because most of these bodies haven't been identified," Marvin Duarte tries to justify himself. This is their third burial in a month. "At the morgue we have the capacity for forty bodies and today we had sixty-five, but in July it was worse—one day we had eighty-five bodies that hadn't been picked up."

"It's not just the fridge that's full, there's also no space in the cemetery," Duarte adds.

Working as the occasional fixer for other foreign journalists wanting to understand and tell the story of Honduras within a week, the common grave at the public cemetery has become a regular stop on my guided tours.

10

HALLUCINATIONS

Light poles are machine guns.

The man with the square sombrero from a Magritte painting doesn't have an apple in the middle of his face, but a grenade.

The bald *campesino* in sunglasses and with the weathered face in Grant Wood's *American Gothic* has traded in his rake for an M-16.

A half-collapsed wall, a rusted gate, heaps of trash on street corners, an abandoned dog.

A drunk, stumbling in the street, halts, surprised to find Mona Lisa wielding a pink gun. He raises his hands and starts talking with her as he would with a police officer. "I haven't done anything, I haven't done anything."

* * *

The Maeztro hasn't done so badly. When his graffiti became famous, foreign donors, always on the lookout for new artists, offered him help. He received funds, publicity, support, coverage. But he didn't sell himself out to the siren calls of political correctness. Not to the left or the right.

The Maeztro makes his own glue, boiling flour and mixing it with water. "It's the best glue, and also a lot cheaper." He prints copies at four dollars apiece. His last work was a montage based on the show *Battlestar Galactica*. Its protagonists were the main presidential candidates of Honduras—among them Romeo Vásquez, the general behind the 2009 coup d'état; Salvador Nasrallah, a well-known sports and television game show host; Juan Orlando Hernandez, the former president of the National Congress, candidate of the rightwing National Party of Honduras, and current president of the country; as well as the overthrown president, Manuel Zelaya, and his wife, Xioamara Castro. All of them behind Barack Obama and the words, "All eat at the Lord's table," and the date of the election: 24 November 2013.

* * *

To avoid getting too close to the hooded guy painting something weird on the wall, drivers make a light movement of the steering wheel, as they do with any minimally different person they bump into.

Painting on the streets is not easy in a country that survived a coup d'état less than three years ago; nor is it, of course, without risk. "There was a time when the police were really after anyone working in the streets." Now the risk has lessened, but it hasn't disappeared. In the end, what he does is illegal. There are places he'd like to paint, but can't. Places of power, the presidential house or political offices. The violence he denounces has also affected him first-hand, but he's overcome his fear. His anecdotes of violence belong to Honduras and its youth. If you haven't been through what Maeztro Urbano has been through, you haven't been on the streets. He remembers a night when he was out tagging and heard the motor of a car slowing down. "I looked behind me just in time to see the window rolling down and a gun peeking out. Without speaking a word, they shot into the air three times. They didn't get me. I was really lucky."

11

NIGHT OF THE FIRE

If something goes right in Honduras, it's usually by luck. And if the country isn't completely shot at this point, it's only because citizens know what they can demand from authorities: after being locked up in prison for seventeen years for killing a man who'd been harassing his father, Marco Antonio Bonilla saved the lives of dozens of prisoners and became a hero.

On the night of 14 February 2012, a cigarette butt, or maybe it was a smoldering match, set a mattress on fire in a dorm room in the Comayagua prison farm, about an hour outside of Tegucigalpa. The fire spread quickly through the *bartolinas*, the Honduran term for the human containers in which hundreds of prisoners are crammed on three-level bunk beds. Within a quarter of an hour 361 people had died. Prison guards started shooting into the air, thinking that a massive prison break was taking place. And then the guards ran. The only reason more men didn't die was because Marco found a key on the ground and did what the guards should have done: he opened the doors.

In Honduran prisons, inmates turn their bunks into small homes festooned with personal objects. A spark on a mattress can spread not only to clothing, but also to a television or a freezer powered by flammable gas, causing an explosion of flame that could easily reach adjacent bunks, often only a few centimeters away. The ventilation corridors between the cells provide oxygen to further fan the flames.

When the fire began, there were only six guards on duty to maintain control of 860 inmates in a space built for 400. Four of the guards were in the guard towers, while only two patrolled the actual units. The keys to all the cells were in the hands of just a single officer. Half of the inmates, not yet convicted, were still awaiting their trials. A few of the survivors I met had nearly been burned alive for crimes as trivial as selling pirated DVDs at a traffic stop. Others, who I never had the chance to meet, were arrested for being drunk in public on a Saturday night.

*　*　*

The night of the fire, Marco had been sleeping in the infirmary, the only room in the unit that was not locked with a key. He was in charge of helping patients who might have an emergency in the middle of the night. His relative freedom, won through hard work and good conduct, was what allowed him the chance to save lives.

"I was lying down when I heard some inmates screaming, calling for help. I went to the key-man and told him we needed to help them, that we needed to get those guys out of there before they died. The guard threw the keys on the floor and left … Remembering these details is a little hard for me. It's sad hearing your friends yell for help. 'Shorty, shorty,' they called out to me, 'don't let us die. Open the door, shorty.' It was hard because I couldn't figure out how to open the door. I could hear them calling me from one place, and then calling from another. I didn't want anybody to die."

"How many people did you save?"

"I couldn't say. A few. A lot."

"How many?""

"…"

"More or less. An approximate number."

"About 250, I think."

Marco keeps his gaze locked to the floor as he weighs his words. Despite his heroics and the promise of a presidential pardon from Lobo, he remains in prison. Which is maybe why he still justifies how the guards acted when they ran and failed to do their duty. "It wasn't lack of courage. They wanted to save themselves, avoid the risk of getting burned." Marco doesn't mention that the guards fired into the air, or that some of the inmates were able to escape their cells on their own.

I tried, repeatedly, to get in contact with the guards who ran off, but none of them were willing to talk. It's easy to

ALBERTO ARCE

imagine the weight of the responsibility on their shoulders. Their replacements at the prison spread impossible-to-verify rumors: one guard killed himself; another was sent to be killed by the family members of the inmates who'd burned to death; another had become a drunk.

* * *

On the night of the fire, not a single prison official called the fire department. The first person to make a call was a worker at a nearby gas station. When the fire department called the prison to confirm the incident, nobody picked up the phone.

On the night of the fire, firefighters had to wait ten minutes outside the prison doors. They weren't afraid of the flames, but of the shooting. It was a question of protocol. The prison standard is that in case of fire, guards should shoot into the air to alert their co-workers. Only when the shooting subsided could the firefighters enter the prison.

On the night of the fire, the chief firefighter, Alberto Turcios, wasn't taken completely by surprise. In 2006 and 2007, he had written reports informing prison officials about the dangers of what could happen if a fire spread in Comayagua. Reports that nobody read.

* * *

President Porfirio Lobo never signed the pardon he'd promised Marco. The law doesn't allow pardons for people convicted of murder or sentenced to more than five years in prison; for once in Honduras the law was followed to the letter. In a country that is able to make twenty constitutional modifications in one legislative session, no politician felt any interest in extending a pardon. Marco has fourteen more years behind bars.

The other characters in this story, especially those who bear the most guilt, had better luck.

Willmer López Irías was the prison director during the fire. He'd been transferred from Gracias Prison after a group of inmates were discovered constructing a tunnel. With the help of a prosecutor, I found that the director used inmate labor to make money for himself. He'd been profiting before the fire and he was likely going to continue profiting in his new post after the fire. He was never convicted of graft or for letting men under his care burn alive.

None of the guards who fled faced any charges either. "If the fire spread in seven minutes, acting with due diligence wouldn't have changed a thing," the prosecutor in charge of the case told me in an exculpatory tone. He defended the guards on the basis of "insuperable fear," exempting them of all responsibility. At the end of the day, you can't demand that any one person be a hero.

The ombudsman has another explanation for the lack of charges: "Authorities who commit crimes are protected by other authorities in a powerful network so sophisticated that it guarantees impunity—through a continued, studied, and professional negligence—to anybody in uniform."

* * *

The media didn't pay much attention to the intricacies of the investigation, nor did they spend time grilling officials in charge. They preferred to concentrate their efforts on fulfilling readers' desires and printing juicy headlines based on the rumors floating around. It's more exciting to whip up conspiratorial intrigue than to lose yourself in the aridity of judicial process, which, at any rate, could never compete with the demand of dramatic coverage.

A few days after the fire, two men who preferred to stay anonymous called a television station and made the following claim: the fire was started by the enemies of a Spanish businessman who was serving time in prison and beset by debt and problems with women. Someone had paid to make the fire look like an accident and get him off their hands. The story spread like a plague in both the Honduran and international press. It's not always necessary to verify facts when every outlet is competing for the same story, when something new needs to be added every day to make sure the story keeps its legs. The logical antidote to the conspiracy theory was deceptively simple: if somebody wanted to kill an inmate, the easiest and tidiest way to do so would have been to hire somebody. A shiv to the throat instead of a fire with hundreds of victims.

A year later I was part of a workshop with other Honduran journalists. In asking them what happened in the Comayagua prison, the most commonly cited explanation for the fire was a settling of accounts.

* * *

To understand the failures in the Honduran penitentiary system I needed to see a prison for myself. Without obtaining official permission, I was able to land an interview with the deputy director, Captain Polanco, of the San Pedro Sula prison. It's not that the interview was possible because of my insistence; it was due, rather, to the authorities' lack of interest. Upon receiving us, Captain Polanco was more preoccupied with the inmates washing his car in the prison courtyard than in the questions coming from any journalist.

On the day I visited, the San Pedro prison—built to house 800 inmates—had a total population of 2,137. Prison guards only provide external security in San Pedro. Starting at the "line of death" (a yellow line marked on the floor a few meters inside the entrance), it's the inmates who run the operation. The guards have only one security protocol in case of a riot— and they've had a number of opportunities to implement this protocol: to back away, grab their weapons, open the doors, and take aim at the interior.

"They know that if they cross the line, we'll kill them," Polanco told me as he chuckled and dug into a box of two dozen Dunkin Donuts (which—like a bad joke told too many times—I always find in police and guard stations). Polanco reminded me of a sad clown on a soapbox: spontaneously and without euphemisms rattling off tragic story after tragic story. The complete lack of consequences Honduran officials face is so deeply institutionalized that many public officials don't hesitate to speak openly about the filth and corruption clogging the system: the pornography of dysfunction laid bare for the enjoyment of the journalist.

In San Pedro, through a huge rusted metal door that you could probably knock down with a few kicks, you enter into a small, boisterous, and practically autonomous city. This is where an inmate-elected coordinator bestows privileges on the population through a payment system known as "the snake." The worst bunks cost about 1,000 lempiras (fifty dollars); sleeping in a cleaner, safer cell can cost as much as 15,000 lempiras ($750). Those who can't pay have to sleep on the floor and do the worst jobs, typically cleaning. Everything has a price: AC repair, beer (which costs three times what it costs on the street), spending a night with a woman, a few lines of cocaine, a joint, a 3G iPhone, or a bottle of rum. Everything has a price and generates some benefit that is proportionally shared between those offering the service, the owners of the business, and, of course, the prison officials, who, as Polanco told me, "contribute their earnings to maintenance and better food."

Housed together with the inmates, sometimes even inside their cells, are raccoons, dogs, chickens, and pigs, plus huge piles of garbage, creeks of black water, as well as fruit and food stands, and shops to buy drinks, shirts, hammocks, shoes, and carpets—all staffed by inmates and by the twenty-nine private employees who enter into the prison every day to work.

This small city, with its captive population, generates a substantial economic surplus. In its shadows a group of "small-time businessmen" has cropped up. Jorge Gutiérrez runs one of the restaurants in the prison, which is clean, well-built, and has a menu that compares with any restaurant on the street ("designed," according to Gutiérrez, "by a friend who knows about that kind of thing"). Like many of his fellow inmates, he has no desire to be transferred to another prison, which would result in him losing all of his privileges. Gutiérrez pays 480 lempiras a month (about twenty-five dollars) as a tax to prison officials, and he employs two inmates as his waiting staff. "Each of them makes 400 lempiras a month, or about twenty dollars ... and, besides generating employment, I make enough to maintain my family on the outside." When he's released, he can either sell the restaurant to another inmate, or rent it out from his home.

It's difficult to feel totally against the current set-up. Without this kind of organizing, the inmates wouldn't survive. "For food, the state allots thirteen lempiras per inmate per diem (about sixty cents). With so little money they'd die of hunger, so I need to figure out how to supplement their diet," Hugo Hernández, a prison administrator, tells me. Like Polanco, Hernández feels secure enough in what he's doing to show us his Excel spreadsheets.

With an annual budget of $18.5 million for twenty-four prisons with capacity for 8,000 inmates, the Honduran penitentiary system actually holds a population of nearly 12,000 inmates, according to statistics provided by the Security Ministry. There is nothing in the budget for facility maintenance, let alone improvement. The only two objectives seem to be that the exterior walls remain standing and that famine doesn't get even worse. The assistant secretary of the Security Ministry, Marcela Castañeda, admitted that eighty-two percent of the budget goes to paying the guards' salary and sixteen percent goes to food. According to Castañeda, "Only two percent is invested in structural improvement." Hernández, the San Pedro administrator, provides slightly different statistics. He asserts that the only money that goes to facility maintenance comes from the taxes collected from the businesses inmates run inside the prison. Is it corruption or survival? The total amount, which Hernández estimates as "about 120,000 lempiras a month [around $6,000] pays for facility maintenance, gasoline to transfer inmates to the hospital or to court, and extra food." And, somehow, despite the circumstances, Hugo Hernández makes it work. After he was transferred to a new post at the Finance Ministry, he was called "back to the prison at the inmates' request, because they know that I treat them right."

The whole system hangs in a delicate equilibrium based on a pact of "nonaggression" and respect between guards and inmates—keeping in check the high potential for violence. Odalis Nájera, the director of the prisons' human rights monitoring body, explains that the last riot in the San Pedro prison just a few weeks after the fire in Comayagua, in which thirteen inmates were killed, was the result of a spike in prices for basic services.

Noe Betancourt, the inmate coordinator in San Pedro Sula, remembers well what happened on the day of the riot, but he prefers not to recount the details. Surrounded by his bodyguards, he walks in the courtyard holding hands with his girlfriend, who's decided to stay and live with him inside the prison. One of the bodyguards, less reserved than the others (and rather morbid, or maybe just trying to test how much I can stomach) describes the riot:

"The last coordinator was too abusive. At first he would beat people with a bull's penis if they stepped out of line or didn't pay. By the end, he would leave someone hanging from a roof all night, setting a dog to bite at their feet. On the day of the riot, people got together and chopped his head off with a machete, and then they carved his heart out, cut off his testicles, and gave them to the dog to eat. They put the bodies of the fallen coordinator and his bodyguards into a cell, jammed in a few mattresses, and set it on fire.

"For three weeks, in an agreement with authorities, inmates maintained complete control of the prison. They didn't give up their weapons or even let firefighters into the prison to investigate the cause of the fire. Since then, inmates have been given bolt cutters to be able to open their cells in case of another fire. They even have access to keys to open the exterior doors, and they've purchased fire extinguishers with their own money. The only reason they don't leave is because they don't want to."

Fernando Ceguera, the inmate electrician who manages the facilities, shows me one of the twelve transformers that distribute energy throughout the interior of the prison. "It's been losing oil for days and is completely saturated with twenty lines feeding into the biggest cell. It could blow any minute." The electrician says that he read in the news that the governor is considering the possibility of constructing a new prison with all-metal cells. "Make sure to write that those cells are meant for animals, and if they transfer us we're going to set fire to everything and sell the scraps for junk." The inmates, according to the coordinator, have plans of their own: "We're already working on the designs and calculating material prices to build new cells in the compound, adding another floor to the church and the eating hall. This way, if we do it ourselves, with just $10,000, we can expand the capacity of the compound by 500 inmates in just three months."

Meanwhile, in Comayagua, one year after the tragedy, the prison's expired fire extinguishers haven't been replaced. There's little that the police detective, Dani Rodríguez, who was named new director of the prison the day after the fire, can do. "The state allocated 180,000 lempiras for me [$9,000]. By selling the burned metal we were able to raise another 32,000 [about $1,500]. And organizers of a telethon, in solidarity with inmates, handed over a giant plastic check that they used in a photo-op, but the actual money hasn't come in yet."

PART IV

THE POLICE

12

AN ASSASSIN

His name is J.E., and he's forty-one years old. He shows me his ID and his credentials, dated 20 March 2009, from the Anti-Kidnapping Police Unit. Seated in a plastic chair, chain-smoking, he refuses the coffee I offer him. Though no longer young, his arms, chest, and hands have that powerful and hardened look that comes from a childhood working in the fields—so different from strength developed in a gym. He's evasive, and doesn't meet my eyes. When he pauses, he doesn't do so to intimidate, but to think. He speaks very little, and in a soft voice. It's hard to draw him out, to get him to respond in anything but monosyllables. He says it would take entire days to relate just the smallest piece of what he's seen and done. He speaks with a certain coldness. He is never, he explains, without his pistol. He shows me the scars of three bullet wounds on his right arm. To keep a low profile, he doesn't take off his hat. He's wearing a button-down green-checkered shirt over a blue t-shirt, jeans, and sneakers. He isn't ashamed about, nor does he try to hide, the nature of his work. If he's decided to tell what he's seen it's not in order to clear his conscience, but because he feels that he's been fooled, used, and mistreated by his superiors. His story is believable, but impossible to verify. Someone had him take a polygraph test and concluded that there were inconsistencies in his story. Which is why they decided not to name the people he is accusing. He wants to leave the country and come out of hiding. And yet here he remains.

"I joined the police in 1993 after leaving the Army Reserve. At first I was on regular patrol, and then was transferred to Cobra Squadron [a special operations unit], and from there I was assigned to intelligence analysis at the National Criminal Investigation Unit. I did detective work, surveillance, stakeouts, and even took photos. The majority of the investigations were focused on people involved in the drug trade. In 2006 I voluntarily left the police. They didn't want to sign my release, and they said that I abandoned them. I handed over everything that wasn't mine: my weapon, badge, and uniform, and I left for good in 2007.

"Months later, in early December, 2007, I met a former deputy, now the sub-commissioner of the police, in the restaurant of a hotel. We'd worked together before on a few investigations. We knew each other through work, and also because we were both from the same city. He tells me he needs weapons and men for a crew in San Pedro Sula, since there's so many kidnappings there, and, from the first day, before starting, he's already talking to me about a kidnapping in La Ceiba that happened three months before and hasn't been solved, and he says we're going to get right into that case.

"It was up to him to find the jobs, as well as bring together the men who could finish the jobs. In San Pedro Sula, everything's fucked. They reached out to three of us who, at that time, didn't have anything to do with the police, but we had the right background. They took me to an office away from the station called 'Northwest Analysis Group,' a little-used office in a region where nobody was doing analysis, and there were about twenty of us in there. The office was in the Trejo neighborhood of San Pedro Sula, two blocks down from the City Mall. It was a big house, with nothing to identify it. Nobody was in uniform, no patrol cars, everybody undercover. Three of us were contracted from outside the police force. We weren't even on their rosters. They gave us unregistered guns and offered $500 a month, plus food and housing. The twenty of us lived together. My nom de guerre was Óscar. We wrote up everybody's nom de guerre on the chalkboard. The same deputy who reached out to me was the man in charge. After the house in the Trejo they took us to a house in Río de Piedras, and then to another in San José. I can show you these places. You put Luminol on the floors of these places and you'll find a sea of blood. In some way or another, the people paying us had all suffered from kidnappings. They didn't know who else to go to.

"Right away there was a high-profile kidnapping that we started on, but we didn't charge more than our usual salary because they killed the victim that same month, December 2007. In that first case about ten people involved with the kidnapping were disappeared. In the first months it became clear how it worked: kidnapper taken, kidnapper eliminated. The policy was that we exterminated the kidnappers. If a raid was legal, we presented those arrested, along with evidence, to the Public Ministry, but only about every ten in a hundred cases were legal. Other times we would detain four, eliminate three, and present [to the Public Ministry] one. When we raided for an arrest we went alone, just our crew; we took the subjects and then we called the regular police and the Cobras Squad to make it look legit, but we rarely worked directly with them. We almost always went it alone. Almost nobody was brought to justice. Any prosecutor could have caught us. We asked for raid orders and wiped cellphones. It would have been easy to guess what we were up to, figure out what was going on when so many bodies kept showing up. Two bright prosecutors caught on to us that first year. There were definitely more raids without an order than with an order, but you only needed to check the names of those showing up dead and the names on the raid requests and you'd figure it all out.

"About three months in they gave me a contract with the secretary of security. They paid me $300 a month there. Every six months they renewed the contract. We always got a monthly bonus, too, some money to split between all of us, an incentive, I don't know where it came from.

"We had to get everything out of that first kidnapper, info about the gang, how many there were, where the others were, and where they kept the money. Everybody talks when they're tortured, that's for sure. We improvised, usually starting with the tortoise: arms pulled back, legs pulled back, tied up from behind—that's how it usually went—roped up to the ceiling so they're just hanging there. After an hour they can't move a single muscle. You beat them with what you have, with your fists, with pipes, with chains. People don't get out of there alive. If you get tied up and tortured, you don't live. We fed them while they stayed with us, but they didn't come out alive. At first we shot them, but there was too much blood, and it was too loud. Then we used a bag over the head, cinching the neck with a cord, or without a cord, and in two minutes, just like that, they peed themselves, defecated, and were dead. We didn't torture them for too long in there. Fifteen days at the most, and then we threw them in the river tied to a block so they would sink. We weren't careful enough once, and somebody escaped when we were taking them to be executed. He got away and then we made threats for him to retract what he'd said about us. He'd filed a complaint to the Criminal Investigation Unit, but we had infiltrators in that office, and they let us know. We would have up to four of them at once in the same room, but as they were blindfolded and handcuffed, they didn't know what else was in the room. Four of the houses were in San Pedro Sula. But we didn't use them all at once, just one at a time, on rotation.

"A number of times we were almost kicked out for not paying, but they found new patrons, got money from business owners. They'd cover our expenses. The bosses would give them a scare, tell businessmen and other people with cash that they could be targeted for kidnapping and extortion. They were voluntary donations, but we had to scare them first. There was a businessman in charge of renting us different cars every week. They came without plates, or we'd take the plates off ourselves. Who was going to stop us? We were authorized for that kind of thing. Pickups and SUVs. We had Uzis, AK-47s, AR-15s, we didn't know where they came from, not even the police are supposed to have those kinds of weapons. We also had police vests, which we wore, turning the patch around so you couldn't see the tags. We also had helmets, all of it was just there for us. I was part of the crash crew, but there were others with less experience, and if there was a difficult mission they didn't go, we couldn't use them. They picked people based on experience.

"Over time everybody had a hand in everything, from the chiefs to the agents. If we needed to clean up a neighborhood to start working, we had to call the local police chief. We couldn't push out the local patrols on our own, we needed orders directly from the chief. And the chief himself made the orders and did the torturing, but he didn't participate directly in the executions, he only gave the orders. The chief had the power to decide who was going to live and who was going to die, and he consulted with his bosses. The chief made the decisions. In almost every operation there was someone in charge. But when we were actually working we were all equals, you couldn't tell between the chief and a soldier during an operation. We were discreet about it. If we were in a torture room, and someone killed a detainee accidentally, and if I said the killer's name out loud, I'd be asking for a death sentence. Why would I risk all that? If I slipped someone's name and someone else getting tortured overheard and was able to escape and leak the name—no, nobody wanted to run the risk that a name would get out. A number of police were killed because of that.

"Weeks could go by in one of the houses with us just loafing and doing nothing. Zero kidnappings. Some guys lost it and went out to kill for money. If there wasn't work, there wasn't money, and so they would have to go looking for assassination jobs to survive. If there was an operation and some dead bodies showed up, the bosses would charge you for it, under the table. They'd take advantage of you, and you wouldn't even realize it. In the end I didn't make any money.

"I was in from October 2007 to June 2011. I wanted to retire, because I was realizing that, throughout my life, I hadn't killed anybody, and I didn't think that things had to be like this. If I'd known how it was going to be I never would have joined. But by the time I had that realization, there wasn't any going back. I'd been in battles before, but I never had to kill anybody, especially not in cold blood. When you're in you get to a point where, with so much death, you don't feel anything for other people anymore. One time there were eight bodies in the house and we had to go and dump them, we piled them into the truck bed, put a sheet of plastic over them, and then sat down on top of the pile. All the police officers recognized us and looked the other way—we were famous killers.

"Those first people we killed, right when I arrived, I remember like it was yesterday. There were three young men somehow linked to the kidnapping of a businessman in La Ceiba. The three of them were all in one car. We picked them up together, and that was when I saw how ugly it could get. Only one of them was actually involved, but the chief said we had to give it to all of them. I'll always remember that first kill. We had it on film. One of them was named Tony; I even know where he lived. Another one was his nephew, a kid about twenty years old, and the third one was related to a soccer player. We stopped them in two cars, one in front and one behind, right in the center of San Pedro Sula. The only one who was actually guilty was Tony.

"We would say that we were the police so people stayed calm. To keep traffic moving. Inside the city we rode with a team of four in the cabin: the driver, the boss, and two more. We were just going to do a stop, cuff them, and put them in the truck. The fella knew what was up, that he was caught, and he didn't put up a fight. But we didn't all fit in the cab since they were big guys, and so I had to ride in the back, and one of them rode with me, uncuffed, I had him lying down, it was absurd, my pistol held right against his head right in the middle of the city. At first I thought we were just capturing them. We took them to the house. We tortured all of them, but only one of them knew why. The money was already gone, there was nothing left. They sent it to Nicaragua with some other folks. We roughed them up to try to get information, bags over their heads, hanging them up by their arms, for about three hours. The chief gave me the order directly, you have to give it to them. All of them. He's starting to act tough, I thought, though I still didn't know how bloody it was going to get. This was in the Trejo house. We hauled them out at dawn on the Omoa highway. They were all tied up inside the cab, cuffed, gagged, blindfolded. They couldn't see anything, didn't know where they were going, didn't know what we were going to do with them. We pulled one of them out, told him to walk. Generally we leave them face down on the floor. It's better for them not to know. They're crying, it's heart-breaking, it's better not to tell them anything and then give it to them at once, one quick shot. It's not as hard that way. Some of us would lose control, shoot them all up, crazy angry people. Some of these guys would shoot them twenty times. If one of us didn't shoot, it would be a mutiny, a threat to the whole group, and you could get killed for that. If you're supposed to shoot, you shoot. That day one of the officers who'd just gotten out of the academy was with me, it was his first day, later he turned into an assassin, but that day he was crying. Since it was his first day, they made him do it. They gave him a pistol, but it's better if the people who are used to it go first, or to let a person volunteer. There's always someone who wants to do it. I made sure to busy myself with something that day so that I wouldn't have to shoot, but the rookie came to me and said he was raised in a Christian house. He was like, No man, I can't do it. He was crying. No man, I can't, my friend. The rest of the guys were waiting for him in the cars. I had to do it for him.

"We were the San Pedro crew, but there was also another crew in La Ceiba, and another in Tegucigalpa. It's impossible to know how many people were killed. In just my crew I could count about 200 deaths. And then you have to factor in that the vice of killing doesn't just fade away. I saw only a few cases of police who thought about backing out, and there was one guy I remember who actually tried to leave. I went to pick him up and brought him to the boss—for lack of respect. The boss ordered us to kill him for insubordination. That was the last job I did, in early 2011. I never knew his name, he was just a young white guy. That was my last job, I did it, and then didn't go back to the crew. I left them hanging. Didn't say a word. Just disappeared. I went and hid. I'd been wanting to leave. I couldn't take it, I needed out. I saw how indifferent we'd become to death.

"I tried to tell a few crew members that there were kidnappers who, when you triangulated their phones, you figured out were working with the bosses. I wasn't the only one who had caught on. A few said that they were retiring, but I didn't believe them for a minute. I've distanced myself from all the friendships I had. We used to go out to eat together, to celebrate out on the town. Now I don't touch them, don't even answer their calls. At night I take the battery out of my phone and I don't ever stay in one place. Two days here, one day there. Always changing, and if I'm in a house for three days, I'm locked inside, watching TV. I can't even work, because if I did find a job, they'd find me there. I'm already falling into a routine, and they can track you down quick here. I'm totally stressed. I hear a dog bark and I'm pulling my pistol. They're going to come for me, but they're going to have a standoff. They're not going to just take me away. It's not going to be easy. I always have a pistol on me. If they catch me I'll kill myself going out. Knowing what they do to people, I won't let them take me. I'm not meant to do this kind of thing, to kill. I was raised by humble people, with principles, I wasn't meant to be like this. If you even hesitate they'll off you, they're always nervous about that kind of thing. Which is why you can't ever get out. It's like the mafia—death is the only path to freedom. The only thing I regret is being needy, needing a job, you think that they appreciate you, respect you, but they were just using you, and it took me a while to realize that."

13

DEATH SQUADS

The masked men riding in a 4-by-4 without plates came by night. They opened the neighborhood gate and, without shooting, fighting, or yelling, took twenty-eight-year-old Kevin Said Carranza, known as "Teiker," and his nineteen-year-old girlfriend, Cindy Yadira García. But they didn't only take them. They also took his home theater system, a music player, and a collection of sports shoes, as well as an indeterminate sum of money. A dog, who escaped as his owners were being apprehended, was collateral damage. Teiker was one of the leaders of the Barrio 18 gang in Tegucigalpa.

Teiker was a gangster running the streets of Honduras, extorting, kidnapping, and killing. He was a veteran with more than a decade in the Barrio 18. Someone who had the final word, who, in gang culture, is referred to as a *palabrero*; someone who gives orders; someone who takes the floor. Someone to obey. I never would have known about him had I not come across a report of his disappearance the next morning, 10 January 2013, in the largest Honduran newspaper—which is basically nothing but a crime beat: "Gangster Tied to Extortion Crimes Falls," read the headline. Along with the text was a picture of the kid tied up and thrown on the ground, with obvious signs of torture, though seemingly still alive. His face was wrapped in tape, his chest bruised, his left arm tied behind his back, apparently dislocated, with an abrasion around the elbow. On his chest you could see an enormous tattoo: 18. The first thing I thought was that that picture could only have been taken by a police officer, and then leaked to the press. The second was that someone had thought to publish it. The third was that I had to dive deep into this story.

I'd been investigating death squads for months, ever since I first heard, straight from the mouth of a police officer, that police killed gangsters whenever they had the chance. With the help of my colleagues—the circle of journalistic photography is not so wide—I was able to confirm, in just a couple of days, that it was the police that had leaked the picture to the media. It seemed that the officer in question was a collector of torture pictures and enjoyed sharing them with his photographer buddies. Sometimes, when they played with fire a bit too much, they made a mistake and got to feel the burn. A bored intern working the night shift receives a flashy image, no editor is around, and proof of police torture lands front and center in the digital edition of the most widely read newspaper in the country.

I went to look for some sign of his disappearance. The officials of the National Directorate of Criminal Investigation recognized that there was an arrest order against Carranza, and that he'd passed through one of their dungeons. Two months later, when I sat down to write the story, Carranza and Yadira were still missing. After the circulation of that picture, they'd vanished. The image only showed that Teiker had suffered severe torture. The pair hadn't been formally arrested, nor were any charges brought against them. The habeas corpus petition presented in Teiker's name was dismissed. They had vanished. The same police office that had acknowledged Teiker's apprehension and had leaked the torture pictures to the press was now claiming they knew nothing of the case.

"At this point I can only think of death," Carranza's mother said to me.

* * *

Gangs have existed in Tegucigalpa since the early 1970s. At first they were merely groups of kids from different schools differentiating themselves by the music they listened to, their clothes style, and the haircuts they sported. Armed with sticks or just their fists, they'd fight for control of neighborhood parks. Their names were *Los de arriba* (From above), *Los de abajo* (From below), and *Vagos asociados* (Lazy partners). They didn't traffic drugs or extort people. The society they belonged to hadn't yet collapsed.

Everything changed in the mid-1990s. The United States, dealing with drug abuse and violence in its suburbs, started deporting Central American immigrants to their distant countries of origin. Many of them were teenagers who barely spoke Spanish and had no family in Honduras to turn to for help. They started banding together in neighborhood parks to look out for each other. Some of them were criminals with experience in the south of California. The old gangs dissolved. There was no interest or capacity to deal with arriving deportees, and weapons and drugs started circulating the streets. Mairena, my driver, always remembers it the same. At first they were just some recent arrivals who roamed the streets asking for a lempira to buy a soda in exchange for watching over a parking spot. Central American thugs. You pitied them, but didn't pay them much mind. No one foresaw or planned for what was coming. Least of all the badly paid, poorly educated, illiterate cops, who were often the neighbors and cousins of those deportees. They shared the same snacks bought on credit at the corner store, and they lived in the same cardboard houses.

Gangs are commonly known as "maras," a word that, in Honduras, also colloquially means friend. That's how they see each other, these insecure kids from broken families with high incidences of domestic violence. In 1998, Hurricane Mitch destroyed a large part of the country's infrastructure and left thousands of children orphaned, displacing families into temporary housing. The perfect recipe for recruiting new *mareros*. If you're disowned, feel you have nowhere to go, see no future, or any possibility of education, and you're sick of going hungry or your stepfather hitting you until you're black and blue, chances are a gang will be calling your name.

The Barrio 18 and the Mara Salvatrucha (also known as MS-13), named for their original areas of control in Los Angeles, started to fight for Tegucigalpa's neighborhoods in the late 1990s. Later, smaller organizations like *Los Chirizos* or *El combo que no se deja* (The combo that keeps on guard), started taking over some of the central zones of the city.

A large part of the violence in Honduras is linked to drug trafficking. The gangs employ load drivers and hitmen from the drug cartels. Often their services aren't paid for with money but with merchandise that needs to be monetized on the streets through what's known as *narcomenudeo*, petty street-corner drug dealing. They also charge the "war tax," the classic extortion fee in exchange for "protection." Pretty much all of the city's taxis and busses, as well as storefront businesses, are forced to pay. Most of the time, businesses pay both gangs. Those who don't pay will die. Recently, in certain neighborhoods, homeowners have also been targeted for extortion. In Tegucigalpa and San Pedro Sula there are entire streets of vacant houses abandoned by residents who didn't want to pay, or were tired of fearing for their lives.

It's hard to find a gang member over thirty years old, as so many die or are incarcerated at a young age, but also because gangs recruit increasingly youthful members. At first the kids work as lookouts or flaggers; then as bookkeepers, small-time drug dealers, or extortionists. The highest rung in the ladder is hitman. As they're more easily manipulated, and because criminal responsibility is legally different for minors, gangs employ ever younger kids to carry out their murders.

Women and children play specific, albeit secondary, roles within these organizations. When a gang controls any given neighborhood, its collective population needs to submit. They must, at least, respect the demand for silence. No one sees, no one hears, no one speaks. These organizations require total integration into the neighborhood, as well as support and concealment—either voluntary or driven by fear. There are no official statistics on the degree of responsibility gangs have over the rate of violence in Honduras, though all the experts point to them as the nation's principal perpetrators of violent crime. It's also impossible to know the exact number of members, but some estimates point to around 10,000. They control practically all the many neighborhoods in the major cities. Even in the cities they don't control, they still have enough access to commit criminal acts. This access is afforded them by impunity.

In the early 2000s, Honduras passed an anti-gang law criminalizing gang membership. The law has been a complete failure. Iron-fist policies have triggered a rise in violence between gangs and security forces. Gangs are also becoming more discreet. The identification codes, like clothes and specific tattoos, can now only be seen in prisons or on the bodies of the most important and oldest kingpins, those who tattooed themselves years ago. Now, needing business administrators to manage the large sums of money they move, they send the smart kids to university. They even payroll full-time doctors and clandestine clinics so they don't have to go to the hospital when they're wounded in action.

During the civil and revolutionary wars in Guatemala, El Salvador, Nicaragua, and Honduras military groups and government policy called for the execution of leftists. However, since the beginning of this century human rights organizations decry the policy of social cleansing employed against gang members. The authorities have always blamed gang deaths on internal fighting. But, every so often, the death squads return.

* * *

To communicate with Teiker's family, I needed gang approval. An intermediary explained to them that I was only there to talk about the disappearances. Once I got authorization, however, things weren't much easier. To enter one of these gang-controlled zones, you have to drive with your windows rolled down, one hand out of the window and the other in sight—slowly, so that everyone can see who's coming. A lit cigarette also helps. It keeps the driver happy and shows the gang members that he isn't prepared to shoot. Get out of the car with a coffee in one hand and a notebook in the other. Without a jacket, if possible, and dressed in such a way that there's no lump around the hip that can trigger any misunderstandings. Then, do your best to find a nearby mother, because no one around here is much help in identifying the house. Ask for the address and let yourself be led. Finally, if you're lucky, see the kids face-to-face and ask them what happened.

To enter Barrio 18 territory is to penetrate a zone sealed by silence, secrecy, and the total control of space, movement, and information. Gang presence starts at the first street corner. They observe me, size me up, control me; they bring me, take me, let me be. They play with me, frighten me, and, high as shit on who knows what, see right through me with their adolescent eyes. They, the gang members, are the state. But it's not only them, it's also their neighbors, their sisters, their mothers. Even the dogs and the stones seem perfectly placed to incite a general feeling of unease. If you make a mistake, if you violate one of the unwritten and perhaps unknown rules, you don't make it out alive. Reporting on the gang is like reporting in a trench full of ghosts—you make sure not to see or hear too much; you weigh your questions, filter your answers, and try to maintain perspective. They're criminals and will probably lie. They're a necessary source, but not a sufficient one.

One of Teiker's neighbors agreed to tell me what happened that night as long as I didn't reveal his identity. He talked because they told him to talk, and he certainly can't say no to them, not if he wants to go on living in relative peace. He asked me, the journalist, for a small favor, to leave him out of everything: living where he lived, he already had enough to worry about.

"It all happened around ten at night. They screamed, 'Police!' and I knew there were a lot of them because of the footprints they left in the flowerbeds. They opened the gates, there was a lot of noise for a few minutes (like they were kicking things over) and then they left. Silence returned—the doors had been left open and no one was in the house. People around the neighborhood were saying that police cars were on the street, and they came in with a key, or someone opened the door for them since the gates to the neighborhood were intact."

The neighbor's version of events matches that of Jonathan Flores, one of the gang lookouts who also worked as a "driver" for Carranza.

"They called me immediately and told me to come see what had happened, because I knew that house. The gate wasn't broken in. The whole house was a mess, but the dog had been left alone. The neighbors told us everything had happened really fast: no violence, no screams, no fired shots. I went in, I looked around, then left. I saw two Nissan Frontiers, one blue and the other white, both without plates. They were talking with the neighbors. There were like six or seven of them, dressed in civilian clothing, with bulletproof vests, body armor, and face masks. All the neighbors were outside to see what had happened."

An untrusting journalist will always suspect that the gang member had tried to leave unnoticed. But the gang member's friend is offended by the question: "He didn't have any motive to leave," he says, "he was working fine here. If one doesn't want to be here, he says so, and he leaves. If he leaves for the States, he says so, and tells his mother too, they don't leave their moms behind just like that."

Thirty years ago soldiers conducting guerrilla warfare organized themselves into small cells. In the gangs today these small cells are called cliques. The logic is the same: establish a network of support and control so that gang members are never alone. Each person has a contact who only knows one other contact, or, at most, a few other people, so if someone goes down the whole structure doesn't crumble with them. If the police take one member down, his absence is immediately detected by his neighbors, the lookouts, and other members of the clique, and then the gears in the machine start turning. They know that if they act fast and find him, they might not only save his life, but also free him. It's a matter of finding the right person among those who have apprehended him and slapping down a sum of money they simply can't refuse. Or, at least, that's how the gang members explained it to me.

That night, Blanca received a call from the gang and, trailed by a group of neighborhood kids, she started searching for her child and his girlfriend. In the offices of the National Directorate of Criminal Investigation she found twenty police officers, some of them masked, playing with their guns. She asked them where her son was. "Go look for those dogs at El Tablón," she remembers them telling her. El Tablón is a well-known dumping ground in Tegucigalpa, where executed youths have been exhumed, bound by their hands and feet, sometimes with signs of torture. Sometimes they call El Tablón "The Dump." It's a handy phrase. Go look for someone at El Tablón is a way of saying they're dead.

*　*　*

A few months before the police murdered her son, Julieta Castellanos, dean of the National Autonomous University of Honduras, publicly referenced a report that decried police involvement in the death of 149 Hondurans between 2011 and 2012. The report also counted twenty-five police murders of members of the Barrio 18 gang in the previous twenty-three months. According to other sources, the Public Ministry had also received 200 reports of cases that could be classified as murders perpetrated by death squads in Tegucigalpa and San Pedro Sula. The reports made clear that these deaths resulted from confrontations between gangs and police, or a policy of social cleansing, but—most alarming—I repeatedly came across data that pointed to the existence of death squads.

"I don't have any doubt that a policy of social cleansing exists and has been implemented by the authorities," a state official told me. Around that same time a local newspaper published a video leaked by the police in which a group of masked men, armed with AK-47s, step out of a car and shoot at five youths walking in the street. Three of them were able to run away, two were forced onto the ground, head down, and were executed in cold blood. One died instantly. The other was still moving when his aggressors ran away. He died a few hours later in the hospital.

Following any and all leads on Carranza and Cindy (Teiker's girlfriend), I was able to uncover other cases of Barrio 18 members who'd been disappeared or murdered by the police. The practice of disappearance was obvious to everybody—an open secret. And it didn't take long for me to get an earful of advice from friends and colleagues. The problem wasn't adding up past events or commenting on the most lurid details in private; the problem was publishing those details. It was best, I was told, to leave them be. Every time I tried to expand my list of cases or get a name, date, detail, piece of advice, or lead to follow, someone would say to me, "Listen, man, you gotta drop this, we all know what's there. Nothing is going to change. For your own good, don't get involved." The editor in chief of a newspaper ended up telling me, with complete calm, how the police had threatened to take action if they were to divulge any fact about the origins of that picture of Carranza's tortured body.

Stubborn, I wanted more. More stories. In the end, unlike the Honduran journalists, I could leave Honduras whenever I pleased. The privileges of the foreigner, however, are also his obligations. People always told me that any Honduran journalist would have died asking the questions I asked, that my passport and company protected me, as well as my ability to escape if things went awry. It was time that I became of some use.

I wanted to complete the circle. I wanted to find more cases. I wanted firm proof that those masked men were police and not members of some other gang. I went to meet with them again. And I made a serious mistake, the mistake of an autodidact with no one to consult, the mistake of someone with no official training in this line of work.

They told me to meet them in the neighborhood. I arrived in a taxi. A kid was waiting to lead me through unpaved alleys until we got to a house where a family sat watching TV. Before entering, I had to let myself be searched by a teenager with a Uzi in hand. I greeted everyone as if all of this were normal, then walked past the living room, making my way to a small patio where I found a dozen shirtless, armed members of the 18s. It was a Saturday morning. They'd been waiting for me. I was protected, in theory, by the fact that I'd written the story about Carranza, but that safeguard felt all too fragile. That phrase in my article that insisted that gang members extort and kill, or any other detail I'd failed to notice, could provoke a change of mood in a matter of seconds. I was uncomfortable. Gang members had beheaded people, though the hundreds of decapitations hadn't made headlines outside of Honduras. I didn't come away with anything that morning. It was a mistake. I didn't even ask them for their names or their status within the gang. They probably wouldn't have told me. I put my skin on the line for nothing. Or maybe just to understand that all of the disappeared gang members belonged to the same clique. Any of these guys could have taken advantage of the situation to prove himself with me, gain a few points in the gang. Any of them might have mistrusted me and followed me, pointing his gun at me, deciding to extort me. I didn't want to see them ever again.

The information was published. Death squads, dates, details, sources. It was all broadcast and reported in the most important media outlets in the world. There was praise, in Honduras, for anyone who killed a gang member, coupled with activism and lobbying in defense of human rights in the United States, the country that finances the Honduran police. None of it did anything for anyone.

1 4

POLICE REFORM

Police reform came up as a topic every day while I was living in Honduras. Politicians, taxi drivers, ambassadors, friends, deputies, civil servants, advisors, paper pushers, all of them would talk constantly about reforming the unreformable. At the same time competing for consulting funds to write the umpteenth report destined to end in the trash, playing the national sport of talking about the most recent bribe one has been paid. And then during national speeches, in the news, at the morgue, in official reports, and in off-the-record interviews, the whole country talked about the need and the impossibility of reforming something as rotten as the Honduran police: a police force that kills, assaults, steals, and extorts; a police force so opaque that not even the minister of security can tell you how many troops there are.

The supposed purification consisted in hauling away the trash, instead of recycling or incinerating it. But, at some point in the process, I felt some shit splatter on me. In fact, the fear that some police officer had zeroed in on me finally drove me from the country.

That the Honduran police force is little more than a sophisticated criminal organization is even admitted to by government officials: "The next thing we know, we representatives will have to patrol the streets and capture criminals ourselves"; "Police checkpoints share the same corners with delinquents, and they only work to extort the Honduran people"; "The police are the real drug traffickers"; "If planes full of cocaine don't land in Parque Central of San Pedro Sula it's only because too many trees are in the way."

A sophisticated criminal and military organization, the Honduran police was "civilianized," or disentangled from the military, in 1996. But their hierarchy, methods of operation, and salaries were never modified. In practice, police forces still function like military battalions.

The typical Honduran police officer is a youth who has fled the poverty of the fields to get a fixed income that seldom rises above minimum wage, some 6,000 lempiras a month (approximately $300). A factory worker or teacher makes more than a police officer watching over a country with a homicide rate 100 times that of Europe. Officers work in thirty-six-hour to seventy-two-hour shifts. Most don't have a car and can't pay for a bus ticket to the south or western part of the country to visit their homes or reunite with their families, and so are generally forced to live many months at a time at the police station. In Honduras, you don't see backpackers hitchhiking from city to city. At gas stations and along the roads what you see are police officers looking to hitch rides and spend a few days at home.

* * *

In October of 2012, Julieta Castellanos, president of the national university, one of the most influential women in the country, announced the arrest of a police officer who had murdered her son and his friend the year before. The officer had spent the year, in hiding, working at a coffee plantation where he was protected by former co-workers who would deliver his monthly paycheck. Castellanos explained that the arrest was the result of a private investigation, and that only some of the facts had been shared with the police to avoid leaks that would allow him to escape again.

If not for the murders in October 2011 of Rafael Alejandro Vargas Castellanos, twenty-two years old, the university president's son, and his friend Carlos David Pineda Rodriguez, twenty-three, both practically children, and the immediate action of a mother who was also a powerful woman—there may never have been an open public debate about security, police corruption, and impunity in Honduras. Rafael and Carlos were killed on a Saturday night by a five-person patrol squad. The squad stopped the young men, shot at them, chased them, injured one of them, and when they found out that the driver was the son of someone important, instead of letting them go, they handcuffed both kids, took them to the outskirts of the city, and executed them with two shots to the head. In Honduras, killing is standard protocol for leaving no trace.

The crime would have gone unpunished if it weren't for the fact that the very next morning Castellanos retrieved video footage from every security camera installed between the house the boys had left and the location where their bodies were found. She found not only that the murder had been committed by police—she had suspected so from the beginning—but also that the officers informed and asked their superiors for instructions about what to do once the murders had been committed. In a few days, five officers were detained and, shortly after, given weekend parole, which they took as an opportunity to flee.

Castellanos then started a public media campaign that led to the creation, in 2012, of the Commission on Public Security Reform and a law aimed at cleaning up and overhauling the police force. It's well known in Honduras that when a problem resists a solution, a commission is created. President Porfirio Lobo said that members of the commission and its recommendations had 300 percent of his support, and that nothing was going to stand in their way. In one of his typical verbal outbursts, he proposed changing his name if public safety hadn't improved by the end of his term. Of course, American dollars would finance the process, and the support of the Colombian government would lend it a degree of professionalism. As many as 14,500 police officers, they said, should submit themselves to tests of confidence: cleaning up the world's most corrupt police force would consist in submitting officers to polygraph tests; if they failed to pass, they would be fired from the force.

Colombian agents led the sessions, which were conducted in a luxury hotel room. "They never identified themselves, but they were recognized by their accents," Police Commissioner Miguel González explained to me at a gas station on the outskirts of Tegucigalpa. The officer had wires taped to his chest and on the tips of three fingers, and, after asking him to refrain from swallowing his spit, he was submitted to a short interrogation of seven questions: "Are you seated? Are you speaking the truth? Have you received money from organized crime groups? Have you badmouthed your commander? Do you consider yourself an honorable man? Have you found yourself involved in major crimes? Have you ever betrayed the confidence of a loved one?" Gonzalez passed the test. Even so, he seemed very unhappy when I spoke to him. "It wasn't easy to swallow," he said, nervously.

A year after this charade, only thirty-three agents out of some 14,500, or about a third of the force, were flagged for removal. These agents had either lied during their polygraph or failed their drug test. The numbers I was able to get from the evaluation agencies made no sense. According to a document from the United States embassy in Honduras, in the first 373 polygraph tests, 142 agents were shown to have lied. That's thirty-eight percent of the total number of officers tested. If we applied this fail rate to the rest of the tests, some 3,800 officers should have been fired. Of course, this didn't happen

The final numbers were revealed by Minister of Security Pompeyo Bonilla: of 14,500 officers interviewed, seven were fired. Of those seven, four were rehired due to issues with how they were fired. "We didn't know how to apply the law," was their only defense. President Porfirio Lobo acknowledged that, of the 14,500 officers listed in the police census, he'd only been able to find 9,000. Details were jumbled, and, not seeming to understand the numbers, he gave contradictory facts. He wasn't even able to say how many people were on his payroll. The United States suspended their support of the process. The minister of security was named private secretary to the president, and Chancellor Arturo Corrales was named minister of security. Corrales' first task was to forbid officers to talk to the press. Since then, there has been silence.

The slow pace, as always, was attributed to a lack of funds. The minister of security had only failed to beg. At its height, funds allotted to the police cleanup rose to only 0.58 percent of the total police budget. Priorities aren't accomplished with rhetoric, but with money. In the end, the cleanup highlighted the risk that fired officers may succumb to the wave of organized crime. Something like a Honduran version of the Zetas: members of the security forces that, once out of a job, organize their own gang and rent themselves out as hitmen for narcos.

The police explained that a counterintelligence group was being formed to follow up on fired officers. And then the group was left without a budget. Aside from the polygraph and drug tests, hundreds of petitions were sent to the Supreme Court and the Supreme Economic Court demanding that the officers' whereabouts be investigated. None of these cases were heard.

In December 2013, two years after the murder of Castellanos' son and his friend, the implicated police officers were convicted. Their sentence was read on a Monday, and the Saturday before, as if to communicate some grim message about police overhauls, the events repeated themselves: the same house, the same group of friends, another birthday. A dozen university students got together to celebrate behind walls and barbed wire what in any other place would be celebrated at bars and nightclubs. It was the same house the son of Castellanos and his friend left the day they were murdered. A twenty-year-old kid—a friend of the boys murdered two years before—left the house and soon came upon a police checkpoint. He ignored the officers' demands to stop, and they responded by shooting. The kid ended up with two bullets to the back. He survived, out of pure luck, having sped up just enough to avoid getting shot again and making it to his friend's house before succumbing to his wounds. The police were scared to shoot at a group of kids hovering at the door of an expensive house. The story hit the news without much attention. No one seemed to ask any questions.

15

EL TIGRE BONILLA, A CULTURE OF SIMULACRUM

I was standing in front of the man I'd spent months accusing of running an assassination program through his own police force. All that time I'd dreamed of looking him in the eye and questioning him. Now all I wanted was to disappear. I don't know if he's the strongest or just the most brash of the Honduran police generals, but what I did realize, standing face to face with him, was that interviews are a combat sport, and you either win them or you lose them.

"Sorry for not having time to run home and change into civilian clothes before our interview."

This was the first sentence that El Tigre Bonilla, the director general of the Honduran police smiling ear to ear, spat out at me. At the same time he was crushing my hand in his grip and, like a hurricane, tearing into the reserved room of a discreet and modest restaurant where, awaiting his late arrival, I had had the time to drink four limeades. That cold and rainy 20 September 2013 marked sixteen months since I'd first requested an interview with him. In that time I'd published six articles in which I denounced his possible connection to various murders.

Bonilla doesn't like to talk with journalists, though each time he does, he seems to climb the ranks. He's only done two full interviews. In the first, which he conceded to Óscar Martínez, writing for the El Salvadoran newspaper *El Faro*, Martínez described him as having an "Olmec head." Writing for *The New York Times*, Martínez later insisted that it was Bonilla's coarseness that catapulted him up from an irrelevant bureaucrat to his position as director general. Bonilla ditched what was going to be his second public interview, by telephone, with Renato Álvarez on one of the most watched television programs in Honduras. On that occasion, Bonilla abruptly ended the interview by hanging up the phone.

"He asked me a question and I answered him," Bonilla explained to me. "And then when he started asking the question again, I didn't think it was worth my trouble. I don't like bias, or when journalists ask leading questions."

The second full interview, casually given to a foreign journalist—me—was right before either another ascent up the ladder of power or, finally, a definitive fall. For some time Bonilla had been hinting that he wouldn't finish his term, and that his destiny depended on the results of the November

2013 elections. If the opposition won, he'd be finished. If the governing party won, he'd be moving on up.

El Tigre Bonilla was comfortable steering through the theatrics of the interview. He knew when to be ambiguous and how to perpetuate rumors through lying politicians or the press. He knew how to cultivate and take advantage of any uncertainty brewing between his allies and his enemies. For the year and a half he was in power, he enjoyed enormous popularity both in the streets and among his immediate superiors, but he was also cause for anxiety in the corridors of both Washington and the Honduran capital. He let me understand that he knew more than he should, and the only way to make that okay was to be promoted to higher office.

"A five-star general acting as director general of the police can opt for a different sort of diplomatic post. An attaché, say, in Chile or Spain, to retire and spend time reading and writing."

"Writing about what?"

"The use of security for political purposes, or my time as police director of Honduras."

"Do you take notes, General?"

"No, it's all in my memory."

Two months after our interview, he was named military attaché to the Honduran embassy in Colombia. He left without saying goodbye or even opening his mouth. The joke on the streets in Tegucigalpa was that he was sent to

Colombia to take charge of the Honduras-bound cocaine shipments he was already facilitating. The official version was that he was coordinating the political security measures the two countries were collaborating on: the narco-flights. In any case, the strategy was "boot it forward" ("patadón parriba"—a football term signifying a desperate attempt to kick the ball out of your defensive zone). They converted the policeman into a diplomat, sending him far enough away that they could enjoy the quiet left in his wake.

* * *

Our meeting, which was supposed to be a quick meal— an eight-ounce fillet steak—in a discreet restaurant in Tegucigalpa, turned into more than eight hours of conversation, which, in large part, was impossible to transcribe: ellipses, hard looks, clichés, silent acknowledgments, and no functioning recorder. The iPhone that I put on the table between us somehow corrupted the file, and I had to spend a sleepless night trying to remember our conversation based on my occasional notebook scribblings. Bonilla never complained about what I claimed he'd said, which is the highest praise you can offer to a reporter's short-term memory. Or maybe total indifference—the worst criticism.

Bonilla cuts an imposing figure: tall, with an athletic profile, a shaved head to mask advanced baldness, and a prominent nose on a square face scarred by smallpox. His voice is like a storm rising out of the depths of a cave, first slowly, then gaining in force and trampling any unfortunate bystanders.

He would prove to be polite, humorous, straight-talking. He would use physical proximity to cultivate empathy, and he'd smile with apparent sincerity throughout our interview, except, in some moments, when he'd lower his voice and spill the kind of secret that "should only be published in a book, and not for years to come." It's the type of phrase that men in charge of national security use to avoid answering questions and at the same time let on that they have much more information than they're actually sharing with you. He would insist, repeatedly, that he didn't feel accepted. He would insist, repeatedly, that he liked to write. He would insist, repeatedly, that there were secrets. Bonilla wouldn't avoid any topics, but he'd lead his interviewer into terrain that gave him every advantage—where he could steer the conversation as he pleased. His strategy: to open up, to continually question himself. He knows he's interesting, and he speaks and quotes with fluency.

"I haven't been able to find Stefan Zweig's Fouché biography," he griped.

The French politician and conspirator, Fouché, is one of the paragons of political opportunism. Of humble origin, Fouché survived multiple government regimes, from the revolutionary terror (he voted in favor of executing the nobility) to the restoration of the monarch (he served under Napoleon). He was able to manage it all by running an espionage network. Two weeks after my interview with Bonilla, I obtained Zweig's biography of Fouché. But by then Bonilla had decided to stop responding to my messages. The book remains on my shelf, waiting to be picked up by its intended owner.

Like Fouché in 18th century France, Bonilla is one of the most powerful men in the country. Although he maintains that he doesn't like the caricature of "El Tigre Bonilla," he himself—violent, rough, and inciting fear—inspires it. And he knows how to turn his reputation to his advantage. Or, perhaps, to the benefit of the powers that be. "The Tiger is no house cat—it can really bite," the president would say when journalists asked about Bonilla. After the interview I came to the opinion that Bonilla is most likely nothing more than a useful brute sent in to lead frontal attacks. In any case, inciting fear is part of his personality.

"I'm indigenous, the son of a farmer and poor fisherman from the south, who rose up to become the director general of the police. I was recruited into the Army when I was only twelve, without anybody asking if that was what I wanted. It was the way it was in a country that hadn't signed the Convention on the Rights of the Child. I didn't choose, and I don't worry about it, or question it. This is life. It pulls you forward. I have sweet memories of that time, because it affected me, and made me who I am today."

Besides this one moment, Bonilla didn't want to discuss any details of his childhood. Between 1981 and 1984 he studied at the Caribineros military school in Chile, and in 1987 he studied at a police academy in Spain. He also took courses in the United States and Israel. He refused to give dates or specify areas of specialization, beyond a Bachelor's degree in law and a Master's in security. Enigma is part of his personality.

"I bother a lot of people," Bonilla repeats, like a mantra. "Sure, the rich and famous don't like me." But his constant harping—instead of meetings with politicians, he prefers to sit down and talk with children, to mingle with people from the poorest neighborhoods, officers from the most remote police outposts—starts to fall a little flat. The false homeliness is part of his personality. But it's true that he's not known for meeting with top officials, that he doesn't appear in photographs at work meetings or public announcements, and can't be caught chatting with ministers and diplomats. He's not even seen in photographs with the president, who, however, does like to drop his name

Bonilla travels with just one bodyguard, who's also the accomplished driver of an armored car he uses to zip around Tegucigalpa traffic jams as if competing in an off-road race. The car is always equipped with two bulletproof vests, and between the gear-stick and the front passenger seat rests a loaded M-16 rifle. When asked about his relatively meager security outfit in a country where even the son of the secretary of state has more protection than he has, the director general of the Honduran police force offers a phrase that makes sense coming from someone in his position, but could also easily be misinterpreted:

"Just like I'm not scared of dying, I'm not scared of using weapons and fists to defend myself in case of an attack. If somebody walks through that door, I will jump up on the table with a pistol to defend myself before the rest of you, paralyzed with fear, even realize what's happening."

Bonilla is a tired man. Impatient, impetuous, screaming at the whole world, though I only saw him scream into the telephone, all the while smiling and winking up at me. A man who—with his phones ringing twenty-four hours a day, seven days a week—can't maintain the thread of a conversation, or even finish articulating an idea. A single man who doesn't take care of himself, doesn't eat, doesn't sleep, doesn't rest, doesn't take days off—only the president can authorize him vacation days, and although he's asked for them, they've never been approved—and a man who has been hospitalized repeatedly, as he explained to me without the slightest shade of embarrassment, for stress. A man who's been under attack from all fronts since the minute he assumed his position. A man who, as he puts it, is trying to do things right. And even if he doesn't achieve that—as he acknowledges—it's because he has enemies inside his own police force, among politicians, and in foreign bankrollers like the United States. A man who—even if for moments he has lost control of his unit— has been able to recover that control. A man who's twice been publicly confronted by screaming politicians—once by the minister of security, and a second time by the US ambassador, whose funding Bonilla largely depends on, or, at least, his elite police squad and anti-narcotic operations rely on, which are the programs that most matter to him. From those incidents he's come out even stronger: the president reaffirming his position, and the news filtering out to the public. He's a man who knows how to build up a persona.

And the persona he's built is full of shadow.

In 2002, Bonilla was accused, by then Police Chief of Internal Affairs María Luisa Borjas, of participation in police-committed assassinations. He was exonerated, but the accusations have periodically resurfaced in public discourse, especially since he was named director general of police in May 2012. The accusation poisoned his relationship, and even the whole of the government's relationship, with the United States.

I asked him point-blank: "Have you ever killed anybody, General? You know that I have to ask you that."

"That accusation is totally false. I completely deny it. I wasn't there, and I had nothing to do with those events. It happened in San Pedro Sula at the time I was in Tegucigalpa. The chief of internal affairs put together some testimonies and decided to come after me. I'll never know why she did it, and I don't want to keep talking about it for another ten years. They brought charges against me, filed an arrest order. I presented myself [a year after the order], they tried me, absolved me, the prosecutor tried again, and the Supreme Court absolved me again. Not another single case has been brought against me. There's nothing on me."

Arabeska Sánchez, the director of IUDPAS (Academic Institute of Democracy, Peace and Security) of the National University of Honduras, and a professor at the National Police Academy for ten years, knows Bonilla well. "Society sees him as a dangerous person," she tells me. "And he himself has told me he's an attack dog that politicians let loose when they see fit. He's introverted, shy, and not well known. A man without vices, studious, a hard worker, methodical. He works night after night without rest. Even his colleagues look at him with something between fear and respect. He's in charge now because he's the least bad option. There was nobody else to pick for head of police who didn't have known ties to organized crime, and yet it's not known—and you can't even openly question this—if he's been implicated for charges of human rights violations. Bonilla is more military than police. He's a defender of the Army, seen by many as the man who facilitated the militarization of public security. He's a man who, when he wants, can be a charismatic public figure, even funny, and yet at the same time, he's a man nobody would want to meet at night in a dark alleyway. He's a true survivor, who doesn't trust anybody. An extremely intelligent man."

Two of Bonilla's colleagues didn't hesitate to refer to him as an "assassin" when I met them for lunch at the house of a friend. The two policemen openly explained to me how they had personally seen him kill someone and then boast about it later in front of other officers. They also told me of other disturbing episodes, without dates or names, and which are impossible to verify. What I never expected, however, was that Bonilla himself would tell me one of these same stories. In that theatrical tone of betraying a secret, he told me how a woman he was attending a party with suffered a nasty accident, "a fall," and how his friends helped make sure that the incident wasn't made public. I never was able to understand the story, however, or decipher why he would want to tell me a story so dark, so confusing, and so full of holes and implications.

Cultivating confusion is part of his personality.

* * *

Bonilla lives middle-class neighborhood close to Tegucigalpa airport, which, like many similar neighborhoods, has recently been protected with metal gates and security guards. His house, newly painted and hidden behind a wall, doesn't match the prestige of his position. It's elegant, but small and discreet—fitting for a solitary middle-class professional. From a quick glance it seems that it hasn't been lived in, that it doesn't get much use. The cleanliness and immaculate ordering of each of the features, which appear not to have been moved in years, suggests the house has become a place of brief passage for the busy life of the general. Bonilla invites me to sit in a corner of the garden that he describes as "a country patio that reminds me of my childhood." It's a roofed outdoor space with a large wooden table, a grill, a DVD player with a small plasma screen ("which I almost never turn on"), and a large bar with dozens of bottles of whiskey and wine. All of it is situated under the steady gaze of Pope John Paul II, whose portrait hangs on a wall. Bonilla opens a drawer and shows me dozens of boxes containing a wide variety of cigars. "People give away cigars and liquor, and this is where I store them, since I neither smoke nor drink." Underneath the glass protecting the wooden table, there is a symmetrically ordered collection of bills from countries he has visited, as well as patches from all the Honduran units he's been a part of and the international units with which he's collaborated in joint operations.

He also shows me his private work space, a small office set off from the rest of the house where he has installed a computer, printer, and telephone, along with a chair and a desk stacked with books. Bonilla is the kind of man who catalogues each of his books by theme, sticking a number on its spine. He marks the important pages with colored sticky notes and underlines paragraphs of interest. In his library you will find exactly what you expect from a general. He is proud to have almost every book published in Latin America about narco-trafficking, from books about Pablo Escobar to Álvaro Uribe, to studies about Los Zetas, chronicles of Central American violence published by *El Faro*, and classics like Foucault,

Fukuyama, Goffmann, as well as many other books about security. He has filed and stored all the notes he has taken throughout his studies. Terrorism and counterintelligence, a manual for special ops, monographs on the history of the world wars, and a biography of Napoleon. In a dresser he has a small collection of pistols and old-fashioned rifles next to a machine gun he declines to discuss. Through another door there is a small loft with hundreds more books. Among all the titles, the one that stands out is a complete copy—bound in leather and placed in the middle of the table—of the report in which he is accused of murder.

"It wounded me so deeply I don't ever want to forget it."

The only personal touch hanging on the walls of his house is a framed and magnified photocopy of a newspaper caricature in which Bonilla appears chasing the Honduran president, the head of Congress, and the minister of security with a polygraph machine in his arms. As he explains: "If anybody is scared of me it's because they know that there's no negotiating or influencing possible, that I do no favors, and don't buckle under political pressure or threats. I don't bend to anybody."

"Sometimes I wake up at four in the morning and sit here to work. At night, when I can't sleep, or when I need to concentrate, I lock myself in alone with classical music," he explains as he boots up his computer. With the same pride my daughter exhibits when she shows me her drawings from school, Bonilla reads aloud the last letter he sent to Minister of Security Arturo

Corrales. He also reads from a document titled Operation Neptune, which he assures me he wrote himself and in which he makes reference to a police operation that, only twenty-four hours earlier, had allegedly decommissioned property worth $500 million from the Cachiros gang, supposedly the largest narco-trafficking cartel in Honduras.

"These kinds of jobs are exclusively mine. I coordinate the investigation, I write the report, I do the editing, I supervise and run the operation, and I coordinate with the Embassy of the United Sates," he says, with a regal hand gesture. "We decommissioned their businesses, we took their money, and they fled the country. We haven't detained them, but we know where they are, in Guatemala, and it's just a question of time before they are captured and extradited. It's the same situation with Chepe Handal [a notorious Honduran narco-trafficker]. We captured his properties and he fled to Guatemala. It's a question of time. We know where all of them are."

Despite the fanfare with which the results of Operation Neptune were announced, a leak from the director of the Office of Seized Property revealed, weeks later, that when the Public Prosecutor's Office took over the accounts they found them empty. In any other country, the responsible parties would have resigned. In Honduras, no questions were asked, no news was made. Bonilla never responded to my telephone calls again. The US assistant secretary of state for Western Affairs didn't respond either.

Bonilla took the office after his predecessor, General Ricardo Ramírez del Cid, resigned amidst polemics and accusations against the police force for the murder of one of the most well-known journalists in the country, Alfredo Villatoro. A few months after getting pushed out of his official position, with Ramírez already focusing on his business interests, his seventeen-year-old son was killed, along with a bodyguard, while they were buying fried chicken in a restaurant. The crime was executed by at least ten armed men wearing bulletproof vests who poured out of two luxury pickup trucks. A few of the men were arrested. They belonged to the Barrio 18 gang. Everything in Honduras is so confused that General Ramírez, ex-chief of police, in an interview in the yard of his house on the day following the murder, mentioned that General Bonilla, his successor, was the principal suspect in his son's murder. When I asked Bonilla, he didn't only deny any involvement, but told me that Ramírez del Cid had tried to kill him on two different occasions: the first time in ordering him to act as chauffeur to a police officer who was the cousin of Lucifer, one of the leaders of the Barrio 18 gang, and the second with poisoned coffee.

These types of accusations are typical in Honduras. It's easy to find police who accuse other police of murder, of working for the cartels, of torture, extortion, and collaboration with gangs. In the serpent's nest of the Honduran police force, accusations are followed by promotions and acts of vengeance. There's a lot of money at stake. The chief of police controls the checkpoints on the highways where ninety percent of US-bound cocaine is trafficked. Same with La Granja station, at the airport exit, where police allegedly rob cars, or other outpost stations where police share profits from drug sales, or profit from the extortion of city bus drivers. All this leads to internal combat and dirty dealing when a high-level position opens up, the whole world waiting to see what the future will bring.

* * *

In May 2013, along with Bishop Rómulo Emiliani, Bonilla visited members of the Barrio 18 gang in the San Pedro Sula prison. They were trying to establish a truce between the gangs along the lines of the 2012 truce in El Salvador, which reduced the number of homicides in that country by half. (Translator's note: The truce has since been rescinded.)

"They explained their viewpoints, told me they were tired of so much violence. And one of the things they mentioned was that there are gang members married to the sisters of police officers, and police officers married to the sisters of gang members."

He said that was the moment he realized how close the personal relationships can be between officers and criminals. A bit naive for a general, that it took him thirty years to grasp this.

"Our police share prison space with the criminals, share neighborhoods, share family connections. The perfect example is the infiltrator who stops informing and becomes part of the criminal network that he infiltrated. I try to stop this as much as possible. My police don't use informants. I don't work like that. If I need information, I pay for it and then protect the person who collaborates with us. I can't be on top of everything, sometimes things slip by me. I'm human. They can't try to blame me for everything that happens in an entire police force."

And yet it seems that he is indeed on top of everything that happens.

And that he has answers for all of it.

The first reporting I did on a case of gang members killed by police involved the youth Teiker and his girlfriend, Yadira. Bonilla knew the story perfectly, and gave his version of events off the record, which now I can print.

"That type of behavior is about competing for territory and the illicit activity between organizations like the Barrio 18 gang, the Salvatruchas, and the Chirizos group. We have discovered, on occasion, that criminal groups have police uniforms and equipment. We also know that there are police who have connections with these organizations. You can't claim that there's something like a death squad [in those groups] because there isn't a hierarchy or an order from the top—at all, by any conceivable means—to engage in illicit activity. Yes, Teiker was killed by a group of police. Do you remember that detective who was killed on a Sunday after finishing a game of football with his friends? It was him.

He was part of a group of police who worked with the Mara Salvatrucha, and we're on top of it."

Teiker was only the first case. I went on to ask him, one by one, about five other cases of gang members who were disappeared or were killed while in police custody. I told him that I had been given access to a report from the Public Prosecutor's Office documenting how a man died due to a ruptured liver while in custody under charges of "public scandal." I showed him dates, addresses, and names. I told him how a gang member was killed in August after being beaten by a group of police a few minutes after he had murdered, with a shot to the head, a traffic cop. To all the stories Bonilla had the same response: "We will investigate."

* * *

Bonilla places a call to the fast-food chain Power Chicken and orders a meal of rice, fried chicken, and soda for himself, the journalist, and two police officers. As we wait for the food to arrive, he takes a seat in a wooden rocking chair and tends to his cellphones. He receives a call from Comayagua informing him that a criminal gang has murdered a police officer. He then makes a few calls and finds an officer who knows how that particular gang functions. The officer is off duty, but Bonilla asks him to join the operation immediately and not to return home until he sticks it to the killers. Next he calls an army officer and asks for reinforcements, lets the local police chief know that he's already coordinating with the military and, between calls, he makes sure to put in another call to procure a coffin for the family of the fallen officer. He also receives a call from the chief prosecutor in the Atlántida Department, on the Caribbean coast, asking for a police contingent to protect her as she makes an arrest, and, after joking with her and asking why the request wasn't made before, asks for her exact coordinates and informs her he'll contact the department chief of police. "If the chief prosecutor doesn't have a police escort in place immediately," he tells the department chief, "you're coming to Tegucigalpa tomorrow for an inquest. Yes, I know, they should have made arrangements before, and they haven't, but this is not the time to have that conversation. Get the escort to her right now."

Among the responses available to resolve the kidnapping of an ex-magistrate in the city of Trujillo, Bonilla confirms to his telephone contact that, "I've already asked for help from the Embassy." A little bit later I hear him say, "Find me that police crew right now. I want to know where they are at this very moment. Find their phones and get to them. You need to have them ask for support from the Embassy."

Ask for support from the Embassy. It wouldn't be so strange but, thanks to intel gathered from the murder of Teiker, the Assistant Secretary of State William Brownfield solemnly confirmed months before this call happened in front of me that the United States would not continue to work in collaboration with El Tigre Bonilla. The US then applied the Leahy Law, which forbids the US from providing assistance to people or foreign military units accused of violating human rights. That's to say, a plumber in Milwaukee will not be paying taxes to fund helicopters that kill civilians in La Mosquitia, or to fund the military training of police who kill a fifteen-year-old kid who goes out at night to meet a girl. In reality, however, neither party is interested in suspending the collaboration. What is written on paper is contradicted in meetings. In Honduras, nobody cares; in the US, nobody cares. A Democratic senator makes a little noise, but his efforts are trampled by the reality on the ground. A legislative argument about ethics can't compete with the importance of Syria, Cuba, or Russia.

"General," I ask, "do you coordinate with the Embassy?"

"I've answered once and I'll answer again. There are certain operational demands, and they [officials at the Embassy] are our allies. Both our collaborative work and coordination are having positive results. Brownfield said what he needed to say. I don't have any relationship with Brownfield or with the US Embassy. Some issues aren't about politics, and you can only solve them in the field. I'm responsible for the work of the Honduran national police because I'm the director general, and I don't delegate my responsibility to anyone. Like Truman said: 'Every man paints his own portrait with the work that he does.'"

The food arrives.

"I've given the orders I need to give, and now it's time to eat."

Which means that, for a time, he'll stop answering ⌣ which means that he can begin a new and uninterrupted monologue. He talks about those who cause the violence, which is an imported problem, foreign to the idiosyncrasies of Honduras. He believes that most of the weapons circulating the country come from the time of that polemical American colonel, Oliver North, who provided arms to the Iranians so they could kill Iraqis, and who inundated the Nicaraguan Contras, through Honduras, with weapons to fight the Sandinista government. Add to this the American deportation of criminals starting in the 1990s, and the disintegration of the Colombian cartels and the subsequent "cockroach effect."

"When you crush a cockroach its eggs explode and the babies go everywhere. Only by fumigating them can you actually eliminate them."

And the cockroaches came to Honduras, a country with weak institutions and a base where they could install themselves and organize cocaine shipments to the US.

"A paradise that the narcos turned into an inferno."

In high academic tone, Bonilla explains how those are the principal actors that have penetrated every state structure, ultimately corrupting them all: the narco-traffickers and those who the narcos use for their shipments and assassinations, as well as the gangs, which are now in the business of extortion.

"We can only beat them if we have the political will to strengthen the police and the Army with methods, structure,

t are not currently in place. Honduras is
ble country. There isn't widespread social
isn't a failed state. When you decide to get
get involved, there's still time, we are not a
failed st... we are a state with serious issues, but we are not
a failed state."

Before concluding our meeting, Bonilla asks an assistant
to bring him a book from his vehicle's glovebox. It's a classic
of military strategy, an annotated edition of *The Art of War*, by
Sun Tzu, the Chinese general who lived 2,600 years ago.

"Do you want to know what I want to end this meeting on?"

"Of course, general."

He opens the book and reads an underlined paragraph
from the introduction.

"We live in a culture of simulacrum, in which nothing is
what it appears, and the reigning vision has no relation to the
real world."

PART V

STORYTELLERS

EL INCREÍBLE

HOMBRE
INCORRUPTIBLE

16

JOURNALISTS

On 24 June 2013 Anibal Barrow, anchor of the TV news show, "Anibal Barrow y Nada Más" (Anibal Barrow and nothing more), was kidnapped in San Pedro Sula. Within a couple of hours a car turned up with traces of blood and a bullet-shattered window. From the moment Barrow disappeared, rumors proliferated. The local press went into a media frenzy for a couple of days, quoting unidentified police sources that "a powerful businessman from the northern coast had paid around $20,000 to have the journalist executed." On 9 July Barrow's body, hacked into pieces, was found inside various plastic bags floating in a lagoon close to where the police had discovered the car. The supposed perpetrators were arrested, and then, as in other cases involving journalists, the authorities kept silent. Had Barrow been killed for being a journalist, or was he killed for some other reason, in this country where people are murdered to settle debt, to avoid extortion, out of boredom, out of jealousy, because of business clashes, or simply due to sadistic madness? As in the case of so many other media personalities, we will never know.

Ready-made phrases: "We're never told the reason why a journalist in Honduras has been killed or kidnapped, which is expressly meant to intimidate journalists so that we don't do our job." "The murder of Barrow was a clear message to all journalists in Honduras." "Those who kill a journalist aim to hurt us all." "Reports of intimidation and continuous death threats make journalists who cover certain beats—especially drug and organized crime beats—afraid to do their job."

Facts: According to Journalists without Borders and the United Nations' Special Rapporteur for the Freedom of Expression, Honduras has the highest rate of murdered journalists per capita: thirty-one journalists were murdered between 2010 and 2013. For two years, people affiliated with PEN, the US Center for the Protection of Journalists, the United Nations, as well as Journalists without Borders would approach me—the only foreign reporter permanently stationed in the country—to ask my opinion. No one ever asked me, however, the questions I ask myself. I'm not aware of anyone having gone around asking these questions, and even if they did, they didn't seem to get anything worth reporting. Journalism has entry barriers set up for those who go around questioning their own line of work. A double standard emerges. No one looks after—no one wants to look after—the journalist.

Questions: What did Barrow say on his program, what did he report, what investigative piece against criminal interests did Barrow work on for someone to go to the trouble of hiring a gang of hitmen to cut him into pieces? Does nobody know, or is there someone who knows but remains silent? He who goes looking will, in the end, find nothing. The perpetrators of the crime were detained and charged. They never said why they killed him. When I wrote that the police had disappeared a leader of the Barrio 18 gang, I only had to write my name in Google to find dozens of links to my story. A journalist's first and last names are often linked to ongoing investigations of a case. When they're killed, the reason behind their death can be uncovered by a simple click of a search engine.

Compared to the overall rate of homicides in the country, that of murdered journalists is a drop in the ocean.

Honduras is a country of generalized death, which makes it hard to focus on subgroups. Journalism is a dangerous profession in Honduras. The reason: because it is generally dangerous to live in Honduras. Taxi drivers and lawyers, for example, are murdered at a much higher rate than journalists. In 2012 alone, eighty-four taxi drivers and sixty-four lawyers were murdered. But neither taxi drivers nor lawyers, nor market vendors, know how to get attention. If, simply by asking around at a crime scene, I can find out why an anonymous taxi driver of Tegucigalpa was murdered, why is it so hard to find the reason behind the murder of a public personality who spent his days speaking in front of cameras?

It's impossible to find any report about a network of drug traffickers—or corrupt politicians or corrupt police officers—written by one of the last thirty murdered reporters in Honduras. Nor is it easy to find, beyond vague, anonymous declarations, an example of a journalist who was murdered for his opposition to the 2009 coup d'état.

The first murdered journalist I was asked to report on was someone who'd hosted a television program guessing lottery numbers. He would finish each shift with a psychic reading. I spoke with co-workers of his who accused him of extorting unwary customers. His case was tallied in NGO statistics of murdered journalists. The last murder I covered before leaving the country was the murder of, according to some, an authentic champion of free speech. He died three years after his last journalism job as a videographer. Shortly after his death, his mother explained that her son had been involved in some strange drug affair.

On the list are the radio correspondents of tiny inland towns, hacked to death by their machete-wielding neighbors, variety show presenters who'd gone around town with an entourage of guards, a traffic police spokesman, a sports anchor shot to death next to her boyfriend, an evangelist broadcaster, and the chairman of an agrarian union: people who, despite topping a list of murdered communicators, hardly did any investigative journalism or reporting. When it comes to indictment, once more the burden of proof falls on us. Did they kill them for being journalists, for talking, because of personal problems, or did these people get swept up in the wave of generalized violence washing over the entire country? Only one thing is clear: in Honduras it's impossible to investigate, and without an investigation it's impossible to get answers.

* * *

Here's a stab at summarizing the situation of journalism in Honduras: insults, racism, machismo, homophobia, extreme politicization, politician-journalists, journalist-politicians, people hoping to become politicians, ministry politicians, owners of television stations who are politicians and choose to diversify their businesses (from brothels to drug trafficking), owners of newspapers who provide the state with supplies and who open and close ministries under the newsroom's roof, along with justifications of extrajudicial killings, source-less news, and articles riddled with lies, errors, and spelling mistakes. A press that thinks it a good and worthy use of a front page to list the names of eighteen family members, all of them murdered and torched in a town where neither the police nor the press have ever set foot. When they, in fact, are still alive. The two newspapers with highest circulation in the country, *El Heraldo* and *La Prensa*, are part of a group called

OPSA, whose largest stockholder is a businessman by the name of Jorge Canahuati, who is also the owner of one of the largest pharmaceutical companies in the country, supplier of the government and, at the same time, the executive director of the Inter American Press Association. The next two largest newspapers, *La Tribuna* and *Tiempo*, are owned, respectively, by Carlos Flores (ex-president of Honduras and president of the central committee of the Liberal Party) and Yani Rosenthal (former Minister of the presidency of Honduras and speaker of the Liberal Party, accused in the United Sates of narco money laundry). Two of the largest television channels are owned by the two closest confidants of former President Zelaya; one of them is even his right-hand man in Congress. Two other politician-journalists, both writing in opposition to the coup d'état, are little gems I'll buff for the reader shortly: Edgardo Castro, the homophobe, and Jose Luis Galdamez, the man with the twitchy trigger finger who resolves taxi arguments by killing the driver—while enjoying the protection of the Inter-American Court of Human Rights. Public service journalism in this country is really just a marketing banner with the following tagline: "Call 2422 with the facts of your disappeared loved one and we will help you find him." Price of message: two dollars.

But perhaps the biggest problem facing journalism in Honduras is the generalized financial corruption. "They offered me money, I got up from the table and I told them that I'd call them, and they're still waiting for my call today," Danilo Izaguirre affirmed, with a mixture of both anger and pride. Izaguirre is the director of a radio program, and, with forty years of experience in journalism, he's found a way to work in journalism while also working as head of public relations for the Supreme Court and as a congressional representative for the majority National Party. Izaguirre insists on his impeccable service. He's proud of being able to take on various positions that in any other country in the world would make it impossible for him to be respected as a journalist. "The law allows it, which means I can do it." He doesn't get it, even after it's been explained to him. He is, he insists, "impeccable," even as I show him papers related to payments made by the government to several journalists in exchange for publicity where his name appears prominently and with high figures. He raises his voice in an attempt to threaten me for challenging him.

The president of the Association of Journalists, Juan Ramón Mairena, thinks journalism has turned into big business for those who are not professional journalists. A dirty business. The state gets most of its publicity from the media. That's why there are journalists who denigrate themselves and let their silence be bought. Many aren't journalists, but mere professional delinquents. And there's proof.

Geovanny Dominguez, the Editor of Diaro Tiempo, the third newspaper in the country, admits that, throughout his fifteen years in the profession, he's been offered tempting trips to Asia and envelopes of cash: "No one can deny that journalists get bribes, and you only have to read the news to catch the preferential bent of one media outlet or another. When you accept a bribe you turn into the defender of the person paying you, and it's possible that the murder of journalists in Honduras have something to do with those bribes. I never accepted one of those envelopes; my face would go slack with embarrassment." Dominguez rattled off this energetic condemnation before explaining that some under-the-table sources pay even more than the media companies. "For a media professional, a salary of $700 a month is very little. Media company owners give their employees some advertisement spots so that they can make more money, and that's when the journalist becomes an advertiser and stops being on the side of facts." That's the case with Danilo Izaguirre, the journalist-politician and Supreme Court spokesman who, as part of his contract with the radio chain HRN, sells two or three ads on his own that afford him "some $5,000 a month," as he himself explained it to me. "The fruit of many years of work and hard-won respect." Mr. Izaguirre sees no problem with that form of "respect."

One day I got access to a list from the Ministry of Health entitled, "Friendly Relationships." In it were the names of sixty-four Honduran informants who received hundreds or even thousands of dollars from August 2010 to September

2011, when Arturo Bendaña was the minister of health. Records indicate that the list's author was Moisés Torres, managing director of the Ministry of Health during the Bendaña administration. Danilo Izaguirre, just like Geovanny Dominguez, denied having any relationship to that list or to Bendaña. And yet both names appeared on the document. The same year Izaguirre allegedly received $15,500, Dominguez pulled in, allegedly, half as much—$7,250. "It's not the first time I've been told that my name's on a list like that," Dominguez says, doubtfully. The Ministry of Health is only one of thirty ministries in the country, each one with its own list.

Dominguez's hands shake as he scans the names on the list I've given him. An uncomfortable silence falls over us. The journalist has been sidelined. The minutes tick on until he manages to regain composure. "I haven't received any money from Moisés Torres or the Ministry of Health," he defends himself. But he also recognizes that this type of payment is normal among Honduran journalists; some of his colleagues take on campaigns against officials or politicians with their only goal being to make money in exchange for keeping silent.

"My name isn't on the list," Izaguirre says before contemptuously tossing it to me. After I insist that his name is in fact on the list ("Read it carefully, please") he puts his glasses back on and rereads it. He catches his name and panics. "I'm no longer speaking to you as a journalist, but as an attorney.

You'll need to have a document with my signature that affirms that I've received money from the Ministry of Health. My word is worth more than my signature, because the latter can be falsified. Paper trails speak ... This is ridiculous." Izaguirre and Dominguez will both end up admitting that the document "could" be real, but they do so while stressing that their names are listed for some duplicitous reason.

Privately, media personalities share sordid details with each other. From spreadsheets displaying fixed payments through bank transfers, to the gift of cars, laptops, or trips to foreign countries—or so one of Honduras' most veteran journalists told me (though he also asked me to omit his name in any articles I wrote). Christmas dinners in which the public relations team of a ministry goes from table to table handing out envelopes of cash on behalf of members of Congress who've just finished an interview or press conference. I spent two years drinking beers with these people, listening to the most sordid details come out of the mouths of colleagues who wanted to tell each other what they'd been through in the last week, without first noticing that what was normal to them perhaps wasn't so normal for me. Of course, they ended up falling silent whenever I started listening.

The purchase of opinions through extortion, bribes, and kickbacks has been a fundamental part of Honduran journalism throughout at least the past four presidential administrations. The list of sixty-five purchased journalists is only one example of a practice that many other Honduran journalists believe is commonplace; a practice that, from within, few are ready to denounce. Raising their voice could mean banishment, their expulsion from the collective. Many friends told me, between fits of laughter, that Zelaya was the most extorted president in history, that journalists would walk up to him after press conferences to ask him for money, and that the president would jot down a figure on a napkin, always far more than what they'd asked for, even signing it so that the journalist could then go and cash it in.

To witness these scenes you only have to go to the "press conferences," and, as one Honduran reporter explained, see in action "groups of five or six people who assault an official with the excuse of wanting an interview, even with their recorders turned off, asking him for a hundred to two hundred Lempiras" (between five and ten dollars). Among themselves they've given each other names like "The Daredevils," or "The Joans." A final comical touch is added when these officials flee the scene of the crime, running down the hall.

Minister of Defense Marlon Pasque was forced to interrupt an interview with me to insist to a radio journalist that no, he would not be giving a contribution to his daughter's wedding. But I also saw the deputy trade minister take out his notebook and jot down the account number of someone who'd just interviewed him, without an ounce of shame. One of the radio journalists assigned to the congressional beat came to ask me how much I, a Spanish journalist, charged for an interview with the king. He repeated, unable to understand my non-response: "More than any minister or president I imagine. It must really pay off to have a king."

17

THE POLITICIANS

Soltero maduro, culero seguro. Old and single, faggot for sure.

That phrase marked my initiation into *caliche*, Honduran street slang. I didn't hear it from two drunk macho men insulting a transvestite working the streets of San Rafael outside the strip of touristy hotels; I didn't hear it from a military officer cracking down on a protest, or a taxi driver spitting on gay couples in Parque Central. The phrase didn't come from the three laborers I caught repulsively, invasively, running their eyes over the body of a girl selling hotdogs in front of the Spanish Cultural Center.

No, I heard the words "old and single, faggot for sure," straight from the mouth of one of the figureheads of Honduras' leftwing political party. It was at an official event of the Liberty and Refoundation Party (known as the Libre Party) in early March 2012, in front of the Supreme Electoral Court in Tegucigalpa. I hadn't been in the country two weeks when Libre introduced itself to the nation as the ultimate leftwing party, the party of social democracy, the party that would lead the country down the path of a social revolution and look to Venezuela's Bolivarian Revolution for inspiration. Libre coalesced the various oppositional forces to the 2009 coup d'état that ousted Manuel Zelaya. These groups of "resistance," were later baptized as groups of "insistence," as their eternal protests grew tired—always supposed to start at dawn, but always delayed for hours.

Edgardo Castro, one of the leaders of this new party, got up on stage, grabbed a microphone, and singled out Salvador Nasralla, founder of the Anticorruption Party, which would soon become the fourth largest political party in Congress. In that pre-electoral moment, Nasralla was the face of the left's enemy. On the offensive, Castro called Nasralla a faggot, and founder of the "tutti frutti" party.

It was about twelve, midday, a time to be wide-awake and lucid, when I heard Edgardo Castro say "old and single, faggot for sure." It hit me like a punch to the face, like leaving a bar at five in the morning when the cold of dawn literally takes your breath away. The phrase robbed me of my romantic vision of Central American political ideology (a product spawned from the Central American heat—"the iron sun") and that romantic nostalgia radiating off the Zelaya sympathizers waving their black and red flags, wearing their Che Guevara shirts, and playing their folksy Joan Manuel Serrat and Quilapayun music. We Europeans in the Americas have no antidote to this. I let myself be deceived by the red imagery, seeing the

248

citizenry marching down the electoral road to power, because, as was explained to me, "This time it's not just about choosing a president ..." I interviewed a mother who spoke to me about her kids' meals. A construction worker on strike who believed in the end of exploitation. Bandaged students coughing from tear gas, marching in protests dispersed by firearms, and discussing pushing back against the coup government. And all of a sudden, when it was least expected, the rhetoric of one of their leaders punched me in the face.

The truth is that Nasralla, who bore the brunt of those words, never seemed to me a particularly serious politician. I would never be the one to defend him as the future of any country. He launched his presidential campaign by creating a political party called the Anticorruption Party. And he introduced himself to Honduras with marathon TV programming lasting an entire Sunday, in which he appeared, at one point, sporting a thong while wading in a pool surrounded by girls in bikinis, and, in another spot, playing a sort of wheel of fortune game with viewers. When he wasn't entertaining poolside, he was commenting on Honduran soccer teams. In the middle of the electoral campaign, before acting as a sports announcer at one of the national soccer games, he sauntered through farmland soliciting the cheers of the masses—those who would later land him thirteen seats in Congress. At any rate, his method of wooing the popular vote wasn't so different from the tactics of the leftwing politician that morning: the ousted ex-president, with his thick mustache, his formal white *guayabera* shirt, and his cowboy boots, singing *Rancheras* alongside his ex-cabinet members—even daring to belt out various songs by Silvio Rodriguez.

Edgardo Castro isn't merely one of those journalists celebrated by international NGOs for bravely working in a country where the free press only exists in theory. Aside from being a homophobe, he's also a representative of the self-proclaimed leftwing caucus of Congress, which promotes a constituent assembly and the refounding of the country. Also, in mid-2014, he was alleged to have been named as an accomplice in a murder. Traveling with another politician-journalist from the coup opposition, the famous (in Honduras) Jose Luis Galdámez, barreling down the street at high speed, the vehicle the two men were riding in crashed into a taxi. In the argument that ensued, Galdámez took out his gun and murdered the taxi driver. Afterward, Castro decided it was his duty to change the future of the country.

Honduras is a country where even politicians on the left use the word 'faggot' as an insult, where fifty-eight members of the LGBT community have been murdered in the past two years. Perhaps the epithet, so casually launched from the stage, helped push the knife into the fifty-ninth victim. It was horrifying to come to the understanding that the left also represented that hate. But leftwing homophobia wasn't all that surprised me that day. The president of the Supreme

Electoral Tribunal, magistrate Enrique Ortez Sequeira, got up on stage and hugged ex-president Zelaya, and said, "We did it." Minutes after his shower of proletariat love, he recommended that I take "some classes in law" in order to understand that his presence there was in no way a conflict of interest.

The first time someone proposed I go to Honduras I thought I would arrive in a place resembling Chile or Argentina in the 1970s. I saw the country in black and white. I thought I'd be a journalist tiptoeing around a fierce military dictatorship, and that I'd turn brave oppositional forces, journalists, heroic defenders of human rights into my best sources. I couldn't have been more wrong. Yes, there were episodes of political repression after the coup d'état: the Truth Commission—formed by ex-judges, a Nobel Laureate, an independent journalist, a priest, and a member of the Association of Mothers of the Plaza de Mayo—documented twenty people murdered in a wave of repression in the year after Zelaya was ousted. The symbol of resistance was nineteen-year-old Isis Obed Murillo, murdered with a shot to the head while he waited, alongside thousands of people, for Zelaya to arrive at the airport in Toncontín. Murillo was the visible face of all the people who died at the hands of the military, those who responded to peaceful protests with bullets.

Those stories are real and dramatic, but the propagandists of the opposition also made up stories. To the detriment of political credibility, they decided to exploit martyrdom. Every day, for two years, I received emails like this one: "Urgent: Resistance Leader is Persecuted"; "Act: The Popular Fight has been Criminalized"; "Mobilize: Fight Against Dictatorship"; and, best of all, "Constituent National Assembly to Remake the Country." Every day, for years, I turned over stones for evidence that would allow me to report on all these grandiloquent proclamations. But I couldn't find a thing, despite my interest and despite the bombardment of press releases from Honduran, European, and North American NGOs. I examined every case, but I could never find enough elements to turn them into articles. Sometimes I was heckled for not indulging the discourse of the nonprofit community: Sold-out journalist! For refusing to repeat the homilies of a charismatic leader who, just a couple of hours after the polls were closed, and with only 2.8 percent of the votes counted, urged journalists to declare his wife president and denounce the "massive and disgusting electoral fraud." At the end of my time in the country, ex-president Zelaya, the face of resistance, along with his fractured party, was publicly banding together with the same liberal politicians who had expelled him from their party and had subjected him to the coup d'état.

At that time I was documenting police and military murders, and also reporting on crooked newspapers that were engaging in lies and extortion, corrupt politicians giving away free coffins they would purchase with money that wasn't theirs, and members of Congress who, from the left, spread homophobic bigotry. All of that was going on in Honduras before the coup d'état, during the coup d'état, and after the coup d'état. The coup d'état, I came to understand, was an event that spun sterile and empty storylines about various nonexistent policies. To the entire ideological spectrum in Honduras, you can apply the following phrase written over a century ago by Samuel Zemurray and sent to a banana company headquartered in New York: "In Honduras, it's easier to buy a politician than a donkey." That rule can be applied to activists, journalists, and whoever has something to say or keep silent about in exchange for a perk or a threat. This is true of those in government and those in the opposition.

I abandoned Honduras after covering the general elections of November 2013, won by the National Party's Juan Orlando Hernández, a politician trained in the United States, who served in the Army reserves as a second lieutenant. In defeat stood Xiomara Castro, Zelaya's wife, the leftwing candidate. The one who opposed abortion in the name of social democracy, the one who opposed the decriminalization of the morning-after pill (punishable with jail in Honduras) in the name of remaking the country.

Hernández took over the presidency with a clear motto and, in a matter of weeks, he'd militarized everything from customs centers to the distribution of medicine in hospitals. "I'll do what I have to do to regain peace and security in this country," he said hundreds of times during his electoral campaign. A colleague of mine, who covered those elections for *El País*, asked the president of Honduras what he meant by "I'll do what I have to do." The president smiled and said: "Every Honduran knows what that means." I hope, after reading these pages, the reader also knows.

18

THOSE WHO IMAGINE

I've met people who believed, believe, and will go on believing that Tegucigalpa, and Honduras as a whole, could, can, and will be able to change. These are people who can't leave. Who don't want to leave. Who leave only to return with greater strength. Who, whether they're mistaken or in the right, will save the country with their mere existence.

* * *

One Thursday afternoon at Cafe Paradiso—one of the last, fenced-in strongholds of liberty—three friends of mine who happen to have been friends since childhood before we all met, reunited by happenstance, got together to drink some cold beers: Fabricio, a poet of flowery wordplay and contributor to slam sessions, has no way to leave the country; Oscar, a movie director and committed editor, left and only comes back for vacation; and Gabriela, a feminist who's spent years fighting for, among other causes, the education of Honduran gynecologists and politicians so that they may one day

ALBERTO ARCE

understand that the morning-after pill is not synonymous with abortion—she is counting down the days before she can leave.

Fabricio, Oscar, and Gabriela are three of the young people who took to the streets after the coup d'état. They continued to organize even when it was made clear that the ousted president had betrayed them, and now they laugh at the lies that come from both the right and the left. Many beers into the night, the three of them step into a time machine, and I don't know if they're laughing at themselves or fleeing the peyote trip from hell that is our surroundings; but they surprise me—they don't even flinch—as they move on to talk about Gramsci and university dialectics.

Fabricio recites verses about disorder, entropy, anything that refuses to be channeled in any constructive way toward any constructive end, about chaos, violence, and the militarization of the country, about generating some type of political activity five years after the coup d'état, about how to relearn the lessons of the unsuccessful banana strike of 1954, about forming a student-led movement that Gabriela would consider successful if there were at least one self-declared feminist. Oscar wants to meet his manuscript deadlines, and I fall asleep thinking of the clouds of dust that swirl around the neighborhood of Canaán, where the dean of a school told me that same morning that ten kids had had to drop out after a gang had extorted their parents, forcing them to flee the neighborhood.

I say goodbye to them with the same affection—cold, formulaic, respectful, and embarrassed—with which I would use at a funeral, and I get back to reporting.

* * *

That Saturday night I bumped into other old friends, Jorge Garcia and Roberto, at a bar. They stood to greet me from a table where ten other people sat wearing ice-blue shirts with the words "Startup Weekend" printed on the front. Jorge designed, and sold to the US, a smartphone app that turns your face into a character from "The Walking Dead." He was doing well. With Roberto and another friend, Alejandro, he designed another open source app that uses crowdsourcing to recount electoral results in Honduras and assess whether or not there was fraud. They only ever left the country to look for new clients for their source code. They explained to me, optimistically—beer and rum in hand—that India was losing the programming battle, and they were the ones who were winning. They said it was cheaper for "Gringolandia" to outsource jobs to the northern triangle of Central America. They said they needed to join forces and think about opening a workspace where ideas could flow, where they could teach each other. The Silicon Valley *catracho* (a fried corn tortilla loaded with beans and cheese—colloquially anything of Honduran origin is known as *catracho*) would make a great story, and they know how to sell it.

* * *

The group that gets together for hackathons, BarCamps, Ted Talks, and PechaKucha conferences—where the tech savvy develop new ideas in twenty slides of twenty seconds each—specializes in the development of digital apps. They've created an app that identifies the phone numbers of extortionists and sends a warning to your entire network of contacts; a pendant in the form of a cross with a GPS system so that family members can always know the exact location of a loved one migrating through Mexico; a cellphone system for migrants in the United States to pay for the water, light, and phone bills of their mothers in Tegucigalpa. All of these apps were created by them. All of them are potential big breaks in the tech world.

* * *

"Don't ask me for false patriotism. I'm staying because I can do things here. We can develop talent. There are business opportunities." Jorge has this pronouncement at the ready. He knows what he has to say. But, afterward, like everyone else, he lets go, eases into comfort, and starts talking. He has a love/hate relationship with Tegucigalpa: sadomasochism, Stockholm syndrome. He's never directly suffered violence, but he knows he's just been lucky. He tries not to leave his house, keeps a low profile, and remembers the streets of his childhood with less and less clarity. It hurts that his eleven-year-old daughter doesn't know what it's like to play in a park, or carelessly walk 500 meters down the street. He's cut the cable, put away the television, and is wary of any newspapers entering his house. When he sits at a bar the first thing he does is look around to evaluate the scene for potential risks, a very common trait of any Honduran. His co-worker opted to hire guards for a meeting about opening new workspaces.

Like any good systems engineer, he gives me the rational reason as to why nothing is going to change for the moment. The argument he uses is an attempt to save Honduras:

"Criminality is just the best optimization of the country's available resources. It's impossible that so many people are bad just for the pleasure of it."

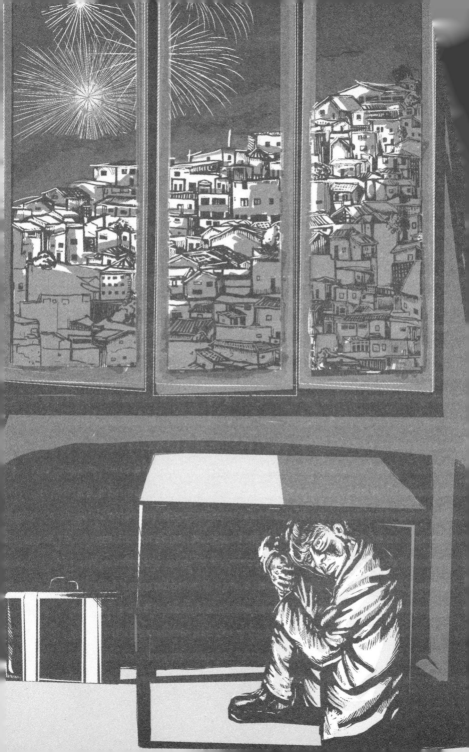

EPILOGUE

WHAT AM I DOING IN HONDURAS?

If the headlines were from Egypt, Libya, or Syria, from the Arab revolutions and their corresponding springs, where, for years, I had been able to show that I was good at capturing the bang-bang, the human fireworks, then what was I looking for in Honduras, a place no one knows anything about, or, worse, almost no one cares about?

I got to know Tegucigalpa for the first time while crouching inside a "capsule" in the United States Embassy to cover an official meeting with Vice President Joe Biden. That "capsule" was a van that, at six in the morning, picked up a journalist in front of a hotel and left him in the same place twelve hours later, with a press release in hand and a look on his face that revealed he'd wasted the day. We couldn't get closer than twenty meters from the vice president. We could have written the same report from Kuala Lumpur.

I had three years to make up for that first botched job.

Between early 2012 and mid-2014, I was the only foreign correspondent in Honduras. I had access to sources, time to make decisions, and the patience to wait around with no greater hurry than if I were on vacation. I didn't need to compete with anyone for the news or for exclusive interviews; my editors approved everything I proposed, and they dedicated considerable time to me. I was deeply privileged. Had it not been for the flexibility and experience of my editors, I would've turned into a zombie journalist with one eye on the TV, one ear to the radio, and my fingers busy cutting and pasting press releases.

In Tegucigalpa, when night fell and we spent our time getting drunk and cooking pasta, we'd play a game called Name That Sound. What we heard right outside, were they birthday firecrackers or gunshots? Were they bursts from an AK-47? Tegucigalpa is the most dangerous capital city in the world without a declared war, or, according to international reports, the country with the highest homicide rate per capita. In 2012 and 2013 more people were murdered in Honduras than in Iraq, even though the population of Honduras is three times smaller. The best thing about statistics is that they offer spectacular summaries of the place where you're deciding to live. They're flashy, but they don't really impact anyone, not even you, reader. They're phrases that work to sell the mythos of the brave reporter more than present any form of reality. I'll never know if I was able to convey an idea that went beyond the number of homicides per capita; if I was able to locate, however briefly, the Honduran reality on the map of the global media agenda.

What little instinct I had was forged in war zones, extreme and "spectacular" situations of great—though, for me, brief—danger. In Tegucigalpa, I learned that knowing how to live in Gaza or in Libya is irrelevant. No time spent or experiences had in the Middle East are useful when transferred to Central America, with its relatively peaceful veneer; where people don't take pictures of themselves wearing bullet-proof vests, but where it's also easier to accidentally get a bullet lodged in your head. There are no snipers here, it doesn't rain mortar, and yet the sensation of being on the front lines of combat and imminent ambush doesn't go away. Feeling yourself in danger during the drive between one location and another is something that, in the Honduran night, is better never to lose sight of. The worst thing is not the habit of eyeing the rearview mirrors in a taxi even when you're going to cover an insubstantial press conference at the Chancellery first thing on a Monday morning, but knowing that your wife and daughter are living in the same place where you're working. The place where, for the first time, those who you write about also read your work.

No reporter would take their daughter out to a park in Baghdad. Why should I do so in Tegucigalpa? And, at the same time, why should I sentence my daughter to live locked in a

a war correspondent? Would a reporter
and bring his family? Honduras is not Iraq.
as a time when I experienced it as if it were. It
ry well be, if that's how I decided to tell it, or if the
media agenda demanded it. It's a matter of focus—fluctuating
according to the dictates of decisions that aren't made either
in Baghdad or Tegucigalpa.

It's true that for now—and I emphasize, for now—car
bombs don't explode in the markets of Honduras. Every two
days, however, people are shot dead by hitmen—a slow demo-
graphic drainage that's unaccounted for, unexplained. Those
killed amount to the same number of people, or even more,
as would die if bombs exploded in the bushels of bananas
on sale next to the National Stadium. The numbers don't
lie. The 7,100 murders of 2012 make for an average of 598
monthly and twenty daily homicides. Eighty-three percent
of homicides are committed using firearms—the law allows
for the possession of five firearms per person—making young
men particularly vulnerable. Seventy-seven percent of those
dead are men between the ages of twenty and thirty. If a man
is younger than twenty-five, the homicide rate corresponding
to his age group is double that of the country as a whole; four
times more than that of the second most violent country in the
world, neighboring El Salvador. Additionally, twenty-three
percent of homicides are committed by hitmen. These are
crimes that have been contracted out to settle scores, usually

by two men atop a speeding motorcycle. Ninety-one percent of murders reported in the country never proceed to trial.

Three weeks after arriving in the country, I covered a ceremony at the capital. US Assistant Secretary of State William Brownfield gave twenty motorcycles to President Porfirio Lobo's administration in the name of the fight against crime. I tried to do my job and turn an insubstantial press conference into a series of substantive questions. It was impossible. A local leader had told me that the local narcos would bribe some of the police agents so that they'd turn the other way when passing any street corner where cocaine is sold. I asked the officials whether they were worried the motorcycles would fall into the hands of delinquents, whether they thought it obvious that the motorcycles wouldn't help anybody if they couldn't control who drove them, if the problem of police corruption continued unaddressed. Not only was there no answer, but, at the end of the conference, one Honduran journalist put an arm around my shoulders and whispered: "We don't ask those kinds of questions here." If I wanted to stay alive, he said, I should keep a low profile: "As a friend, I'm telling you to stay quiet, for your own good." He sold it to me as a piece of advice, but, in reality, it was a threat, and it wasn't made by a police officer or government official, but by a journalist.

A few months later, I was in a hurry after having paid my phone bill at the mall. I called Mairena, my trusted taxi driver.

"Could you come get me at the mall, Mairena?"

"Well, I'm pretty far. It'll take me thirty minutes. Wait for me there."

"No, don't worry about it. I'll grab a taxi. I'm in a hurry."

Fifty meters from the door, someone on a motorcycle got close to my driver's window and screamed at me: "giveme-yourfuckingphoneorI'llkillyou." He then repeated, "I'll kill you. I'll kill you."

I didn't wait. I opened the door and ran off back in the direction of the mall. Luckily, he didn't shoot. Putting your life on the line for a phone is one of the dumbest things one can do. When I got back home, I wrote:

"I've dreamed of this scene, both while sleeping and awake, for many months now. If I were to die here, it would be on a Tuesday, midmorning, I'd be smoking a Marlboro and sitting next to my driver, with my right arm out the window, waiting for a light to turn green and running late to a pointless press conference. My blood would splatter over the taxi seat, my twisted body would make an image no one would want to remember as mine, and, probably, it would never be known why a hitman got hold of me from behind, emptying his clip before accelerating and losing himself amongst the traffic. Maybe I wouldn't even be able to catch his face before he finished the job, let alone open the door and run away. The next day a somewhat sizable article—the European is always worth more than the local—would be published, recounting the facts, giving some context to the most dangerous country in the world, without explaining the real motives that led to the violence perpetrated against me; my friends would write two or three columns, talking about me in the past tense and, in various indistinguishable ways, they would dissect the many floating rumors and hypotheses. Had I been investigating something I hadn't been able to publish, did I have outstanding debts, had they tried to steal my iPhone, or had I acquired some enemies because of some drama with a woman? All of that would be false, and the Honduran police would detain a couple of usual suspects, petty delinquents, and expose them before the press and pin them with murder charges so they could rid themselves of the weight of responsibility riding their backs. Maybe, on some anniversary, someone would ask after the brains behind the crime, but they'd never be identified, and that'd be the end of the story. I don't think I've come here to die. But it's all the same. I'm more and more scared to die here."

The problem, in the end, isn't just that they'll break me or break someone close to me—my wife or my daughter—because of a mistake, because of a theft, or just because, because they'd been sent to go after me, but the problem is that I'll infect my sources with more risk than they've already assumed on a daily basis simply by helping me out. I've learned to understand Facebook messages in which people who'd freely spoken with me, notebook in hand, now retracted everything they'd said, afraid for their lives, afraid that their names would appear in an article. They'd tell me that quoting them put their lives in danger, and they'd blame me for "anything that might happen to them," which, in 2013, was one of the most common phrases in Honduras.

One day, after four or five long interviews, two officials awoke from a long daydream and realized they were, in effect, telling me that the police uses death squads in a campaign of social cleansing. Shortly after I'd written all the details and was ready for publication, they called me.

"Come see us on Monday at eight in the morning, and don't even think about publishing before Monday."

"I'll be there."

The conversation was easy, flowing.

"Dear Albert," as that official liked to call me, "you can do whatever you like with your life, but know that if you quote us they can kill us both. So, please, I ask you to abstain from using our names."

"Of course, officer."

I constantly watched the rearview mirrors of Mairena's car to see if some assassin motorcycle was tailing us, which would mean that I'd lost the battle. In the end, I did lose, and I threw in the towel. A year after moving to Tegucigalpa, my wife and daughter left me. It was the right choice. Nothing should happen to them because of me. They left and I was left alone to finish the work I had committed to: to write about Honduras.

I lasted another year there without them, in fits and starts counting down the days, first suffering the transformation of my house into an office, and then my office into a bar, fighting against addictions, sadness, and depression—a fight I believe I won. But only because each morning I counted down days until I could leave.

ABOUT THE AUTHOR AND TRANSLATORS

Alberto Arce is a Knight Wallace Fellow at the University of Michigan. He joined the Associated Press (AP) in February 2012 as a correspondent in Honduras, where for several years he was the only foreign correspondent to report from Tegucigalpa. He later joined AP's Mexico City bureau, where he continued to cover Central America before going to *The New York Times* as an editor. He won the 2012 Rory Peck award for his coverage of the battle for Misrata during the Libyan civil war, and has also reported from Lebanon, Iraq, Afghanistan, Iran, and Syria. This is his second book after "Misrata calling," Libros del Ko, Spain, 2011.

John Washington is a journalist, novelist, and translator. **Daniela Ugaz** is a translator and law student at New York University. They have previously translated *The Beast: Riding the Rails and Dodging Narcos on the Migrant Trail*, by Óscar Martínez

ABOUT THE ILLUSTRATOR

Germán Andino was born in San Pedro Sula in 1984. He writes about and draws the street gangs, soccer gangs, the mechanic reminiscing about a bygone era, or other Hondurans who write about the reality. He studied at the National School of Fine Arts and Systems Engineering.

ZED

Zed is a platform for marginalised voices across the globe.

It is the world's largest publishing collective and a world leading example of alternative, non-hierarchical business practice.

It has no CEO, no MD and no bosses and is owned and managed by its workers who are all on equal pay.

It makes its content available in as many languages as possible.

It publishes content critical of oppressive power structures and regimes.

It publishes content that changes its readers' thinking.

It publishes content that other publishers won't and that the establishment finds threatening.

It has been subject to repeated acts of censorship by states and corporations.

It fights all forms of censorship.

It is financially and ideologically independent of any party, corporation, state or individual.

Its books are shared all over the world.

www.zedbooks.net
@ZedBooks